Charlotte Warr Andersen

One Line at a Time, Encore

35 NEW GEOMETRIC MACHINE-QUILTING DESIGNS

C&T PUBLISHING

Text copyright © 2011 by Charlotte Warr Andersen

Photography and Artwork copyright © 2011 by C&T Publishing, Inc.

Publisher: Amy Marson

Creative Director: Gailen Runge

Acquisitions Editor: Susanne Woods

Editor: Liz Aneloski

Production Editor: Alice Mace Nakanishi

Technical Editors: Helen Frost and Teresa Stroin

Cover Designer: Kris Yenche

Book Designer: Kerry Graham

Production Coordinator: Jenny Leicester

Photography by Christina Carty-Francis and Diane Pedersen of C&T Publishing, Inc., unless otherwise noted

Published by C&T Publishing, Inc., P.O. Box 1456, Lafayette, CA 94549

Library of Congress Cataloging-in-Publication Data

Andersen, Charlotte Warr, 1952-

 One line at a time, encore : 35 new geometric machine-quilting designs / Charlotte Warr Andersen.

  p. cm.

ISBN 978-1-60705-266-1 (soft cover)

1. Patchwork--Patterns. 2. Machine quilting--Patterns. I. Title.

TT835.A493572 2012

746.46'041--dc22

                          2011010500

Printed in China

10 9 8 7 6 5 4 3 2 1

Contents

Dedication

To all women who, in spite of their daily problems and sorrows, still manage to bring forth beautiful, heartfelt, and artistic quilts in fulfillment of their creative needs. And to the members of my family who have supported me in their own ways in my endeavors—I love you all.

Acknowledgments

For their infinite (well, almost) patience and for their help in bringing this book to fruition, I'd like to thank Liz Aneloski, Sandy Peterson, Helen Frost, Teresa Stroin, Jenny Leicester, and the rest of the fabulous staff at C&T Publishing. I'm also grateful to the wonderful quilters who were willing to devote time to quilt their quilts in a manner that shows the usefulness and beauty of the patterns herein.

Introduction

My original book, *One Line at a Time*, has been available for a couple of years now. Since its publication I just haven't been able to stop coming up with more and more patterns that I can structure without having to mark the quilting pattern on the fabric. I find that I really enjoy working this way and have little interest in doing patterns that I have to mark.

I've taught many classes using this technique, and almost every student has been amazed at what can be done by breaking a pattern down to its basic structure and then stitching it one line at a time. In class I usually start the students out with straight-line walking-foot patterns. They love these, but I find that many students are still intimidated by patterns that use free-motion quilting—the ones where they actually have to guide the needle around curves. After trying a few of those, they want to go back to their walking foot.

There are plenty of walking-foot patterns in this book, but there are also some that will need the free-motion foot. These patterns do need a steady hand and good control. My best suggestion is to keep practicing. I still bobble once in a while, but the bobbles are seldom egregious enough that I feel the need to take them out. It's much easier to work on small pieces when you're practicing—I've found 10½" squares to be perfect for my samples. When I've had several days off from machine quilting, I find that I really do need to warm up. My steadiness definitely improves after I've been at it for a quarter of an hour.

Just when I thought I'd run out of basic ideas for ways to structure geometric patterns, I spotted several more in the background of a TV show the other night. There were window grates in the wall. I had to find the episode on my computer, pause it, and take photos.

So, the design possibilities just might be never ending.

CHAPTER I

Machine Quilting Basics

Test First

The stitches I apply to my machine-quilted quilt need to have the best appearance possible. Many factors can contribute to the quality of the stitches I make, and they can change from day to day even though I am using exactly the same equipment. Granted, they don't change much, but things do change. It is always wise to prepare a large (10½″ × 10½″ is suggested) quilt sandwich to test how the stitches are looking. This mini quilt should be prepared with the same types of fabrics and batting as will be used in the quilt you are about to quilt. Then, stitch some test patterns on this trial piece before ever stitching on your real piece.

Sewing Machines and Accessories

Your machine should be in good running order. Clean it as per your machine manual's instructions, and oil it if necessary. If you haven't had it serviced in a long time, now might be the time to do it.

It is vital to have a well-running sewing machine when machine quilting. If you are shopping for a new machine, take a sample quilt sandwich to the dealer or store and ask if you can give the machine a test drive. There are many less-expensive machines that stitch well, so you don't necessarily have to spend a lot of money. Though not necessary, it is very helpful to have a needle-up/needle-down feature. The ability to stop with the needle down helps keep wobbly stitches out of your quilting.

For the processes in this book, the accessories can be very important. A walking or even-feed foot is very helpful. This presser foot allows for layers and thickness to feed under the foot without the layers shifting and is vital when doing straight lines. I have students who come to class with no walking foot, and they are able to handle the process. But those who have this foot obtain much better results.

Guides that can determine the width between lines of stitching are also important; these guides attach to the foot or machine. The measurements on the stitch plate disappear once the quilt is on top of it, so they do no good for this process.

Bernina walking foot with seam guides

You also need a presser foot suitable for free-motion quilting. I prefer the Bernina #29 foot, which, in my opinion, gives the most visibility when moving a quilt beneath the machine.

Bernina #29 foot

A Bernina #24 works, but I've found that the #29 foot works better with the label-paper templates.

NEEDLES

I have a guilty confession. I am not really very conscientious when it comes to the needle in the machine. I do purchase good-quality needles, and I have many types—universal, quilting, embroidery, metallic, and so on. But I am willing to give whatever needle is already in the machine a trial before I change it. It may have been a needle I was mending jeans with the day before, but I'm willing to thread my machine and have a go at my test sample before I change the needle. If the stitches look good with that needle, I'll use it. But if they don't look right, the needle is the first thing I'll change, and I will probably use a needle that is designated for quilting in a size to match the type of thread that I'm using.

There is one exception to this casual philosophy of mine, though. If I plan to quilt with metallic thread, I have learned from experience that I will need to use a topstitching needle or a metallic needle in order to get good stitches with little breakage.

Batting

A low-loft (thinner) batting is always preferable for machine quilting. High-loft batting is only suitable for tying quilts and is almost impossible to feed through a home sewing machine. There are several types of batting—cotton, wool, polyester, and blends. I have had success and disappointment with various battings, so be sure to use the mini test quilt to try out the performance of the batting. No matter how much you test, though, sometimes problems don't become apparent until after the quilt is finished, such as when a batting beards.

Most of the time, I prefer batting with all, or mostly, natural fibers. These types seem to cling to the top and backing of the quilt, so less slippage occurs. I have been using the new bamboo and bamboo-blend batting lately, with good results.

Basting the Quilt Sandwich

There are a variety of ways to hold the top, batting, and backing together. Some quilters prefer to pin baste, but I find the pins too obtrusive and not that quick to remove. I prefer to thread baste. If the quilt is large, I stretch it in a frame. If it is a small piece, I lay it on a table with a cutting mat under it to protect the tabletop. I use a 3″-long soft sculpture needle filled with polyester cone thread (inexpensive stuff) and crosshatch the quilt with 1″-long stitches—rows that run horizontally and vertically and are about 3″ to 4″ apart.

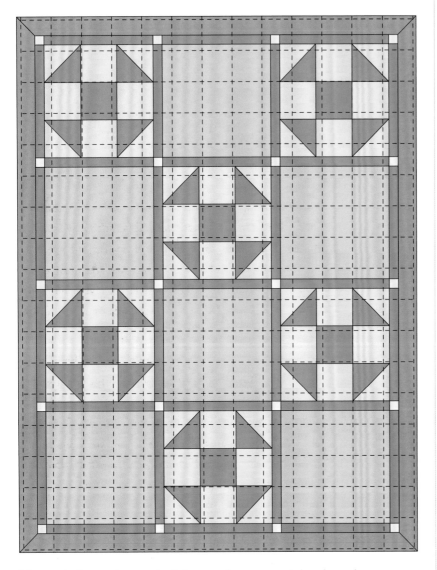

These stitches and rows don't have to be very straight; the only purpose they serve is to hold the quilt together until an area is quilted. If the presser foot gets caught under one of these basting threads, there is enough quilting to hold the quilt together, so just snip the thread with scissors. Once an area has been quilted, it's easy to pull out the basting thread unless the quilting is very dense. If the quilting will be dense, remove some of the basting thread before quilting in that area.

You may also want to try an adhesive spray to hold the layers together. Personally, I don't like working with these sprays a lot, but I have used them occasionally. Try to use the spray outdoors because you don't want the floating particles in your lungs.

Another alternative is fusible batting, which I used to make the small samples for this book and the first book, *One Line at a Time*. Be sure to test first, because when I used them, one brand worked acceptably and with another the fusible component of the batting bled through to the surface of the fabric and made horrible stains. I like the light adhesive on Mountain Mist fusible batting, but it's so light that it doesn't stick very well to some fabrics that have a lot of finish.

In my experience, it was difficult to keep the quilt flat while fusing the layers together on an ironing board, so it seemed difficult to use this batting in a large quilt. You might have more success with this batting if you have a large flat surface that can be safely ironed on.

Threads

A wonderful variety of threads

There are many types of thread available for machine quilting, and what to use is a matter of preference. Thick, heavy threads make a very visible impact on the quilt; variegated threads create subtle movement for the eye; metallics add a lovely sparkle; and fine machine embroidery threads can be used for quilting, creating delicate lines. The most important criterion is that the thread be of good quality and have little breakage—there is nothing more frustrating than a thread that constantly snaps.

Truthfully, you can use just about any thread (with a few exceptions, such as fusible thread) that you can get your hands on for machine quilting. But it also seems true that you do get what you pay for—inexpensive thread does not always perform well.

Thread does not have to say "machine quilting" in order to be used for machine quilting. Of course, some threads will work better than others. Although you can use hand-quilting thread in a machine, it does not always feed through well or give the best-looking stitch. But then, I've used some machine quilting threads that were labeled as such and they were awful in my machine. I've had friends recommend a thread for quilting that they said worked wonderfully in their machines and looked great on their quilts, but when I used it with my machines (higher-end Berninas), the thread performed abysmally in both of them. So, I just have to tell you to try a thread and see how it works for you.

For the most part, I prefer cotton threads. They perform best in my machines and seem to play well with the fabrics I use. I have also used polyester threads with great success. I like the look of rayon and have used it with favorable results, but it is a bit slippery and I worry about knots coming loose. For a truly impressive look, I adore metallic threads and prefer Superior Threads metallics.

Most of the time when I quilt, I use the same thread in the bobbin as in the top of the machine. Though my machines are both quality ladies and great performers, and I think I have the tension adjusted well on them, every once in a while they will throw a less-than-desirable stitch. If I'm using the same thread on the top and bottom, the imperfect stitch is usually not a problem.

Thread Tension and Stitch Length

Ideally, when machine quilting, the thread tension should be balanced, so when the top thread and the bobbin thread meet there is an even amount of each thread. Loops that come through to the front or the back of the quilt are unattractive. Balance can be achieved by working with either the tension control for the top thread or adjusting the tension screw on the bobbin. Refer to your machine manual for instructions for doing this. It is easier to work with the top thread tension control first to see if you can get a desirable balance. The tension screw on the bobbin is a bit more delicate to work with. If you must turn it, think of the hour marks on a clock—only turn the bobbin screw one hour at a time.

Stitch length largely depends on the desired look. Tiny stitches don't look good if done in a heavy thread. The finer the thread, the smaller the stitches can be. Most of the time when using a walking foot, I use the default stitch length (usually 2.2) of my machine. But if the quilt is small scale and I'm using embroidery thread for quilting, I will decrease the stitch length.

Some of the patterns in this book are so angularly geometric that it is possible to count the number of stitches between corners. In this case, it is possible to adjust the stitch length to suit counting stitches.

Machine Quilting Aids

Machine quilting aids

There are many products on the market designed to help with machine quilting. They seem to fall into two categories:

- Items that improve grip on the quilt while moving it
- Items that improve the surface over which the quilt must be moved

Some of the products I have tried that improve grip on the quilt while moving it are the following:

- Clover Non Slip Finger, a gluestick-like substance that you apply to your fingertips
- Neutrogena Hand Cream, which gives a slight amount of tack to your hands
- Machingers gloves

These products are all helpful, but their usefulness may also depend on how comfortable they are for you. I like Machingers most of the time, except when the weather is hot and humid and I would rather have my hands bare; then I resort to one of the other products mentioned.

Items that improve the surface over which the quilt must be moved include the following:

- At least two kinds of silicone sheets that can be applied to the table of the machine to help the quilt glide somewhat easier

- An aerosol product called Quilt Glide that can be sprayed on the surface of the machine table

Speaking of surfaces, the biggest help to machine quilting is a cabinet for the machine with a large, level surface that can support most, if not all, of a quilt. Having to pull the quilt up over the corners of a small quilting surface creates a lot of drag—both on your quilting lines, causing inaccuracies, and on your shoulders.

Pattern Templates

For several of the patterns in this book, you will need to make a template on a full-sheet label. These labels are available at your local office supply store (Office Max, Staples, Office Depot, etc.) under the Avery brand or sometimes under that particular store's brand. Copy the patterns onto the label paper, preferably in color. Cut on the black line unless otherwise specified.

Tip

If after using this technique you decide you want to use it a lot, you may want to purchase these full-sheet sticky labels in bulk. The least expensive place I have found to purchase them is OnlineLabels.com, where you can get them in packages of 100 sheets.

The labels are letter size, so you are limited to the length of the paper. However, you can cut out several and stick them together, aligning the shapes, to form a long template. After cutting a template out, if there are no seams to peel off the paper backing, stick a pin

into the backing paper about ¼" from the edge and pointing back to the edge. This will usually make a small separating split, making it easy to peel off the backing paper.

These templates can be used over and over until they lose their stickiness. If the template hangs off an edge of the quilt, be sure the template doesn't stick to the surface of the table, because it will probably stick better to the table than to the fabric.

Depending on the foot you are using, the edge of the foot may get caught under the sticky template if the template is not stuck down evenly. If the foot goes under, stop with the needle down and lift the presser foot and place it on top.

I feel comfortable using the adhesive on these templates on my quilts. I have used them on silk with no lasting or harmful effects that I can see. I would advise that you not leave the templates on the fabric for long periods of time, however, as it gives the adhesive more time to absorb into the fabric.

Centering Designs

If you wish to center the design, score a line in the center of the area to be quilted by marking against a ruler with a tapestry needle. This forms a slight crease in the fabric. Some designs need both vertical and horizontal score lines. Note: Some of the patterns call for score lines that are ½" from the center.

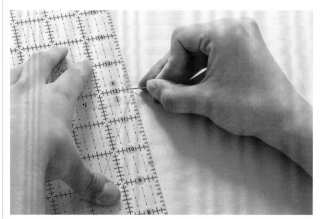

Score vertical line.

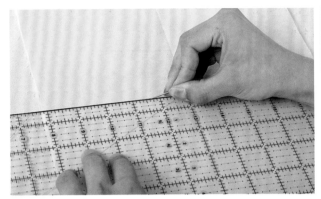
Score horizontal line.

Continuous Lines

The fewer starts and stops that are made when machine quilting, the less tidying up needs to be done. This is why continuous lines are desirable. Some designs and patterns are naturally continuous; some have to have continuity built into them. Continuity can also be created by backtracking over previous stitching—I call this overstitching. But overstitching can cause a heavy look from a buildup of thread or from inaccuracy when stitching over previous threads. It all depends on the look you want. If I feel that an accumulation of thread will be distracting, I am perfectly willing to do the extra finishing work required by more starts and stops.

Where Geometry and Free Forms Entwine

As a quilting line comes to the edge of a shape, you may want to stop and end the line there, or, for continuity's sake, you may choose to stitch along the edge of the shape to where the next line of the quilting pattern may be picked up. I have found that I mostly prefer to stop and tie the ends off rather than overstitch. If there is a great deal of thread built up, that thread becomes much too visible. But if I feel that the extra layer of thread will be subtle enough, I will stitch over the top of existing thread.

Once a quilt top has been completed, the most difficult decision becomes how to quilt it—what patterns to use, the scale of those patterns, how to make them enhance the design of the top, and how to make them an integral and important part of the whole quilt. The patterns that I have offered for your use in this book can be used in all types of quilts and, when placed well, can spotlight the elements of the top.

Completing Interrupted Lines

When quilting lines come up against shapes such as appliqué, the lines are interrupted and it can be hard to determine how to complete the pattern, especially since we're trying to avoid marking the quilt. As I come to these shapes, I try to visualize what the fragmented edges of the pattern look like and finish the lines accordingly. These fragments might not always be quite true to the geometry of the pattern, though. If perfect lines are needed, it may help to make an overlay of the pattern. Draw a repeat or two of the pattern to scale on a piece of write-on transparency film or see-through vinyl. This overlay can then be placed on top of the area where the quilting pattern is interrupted, and then the fragmented lines can be completed almost perfectly.

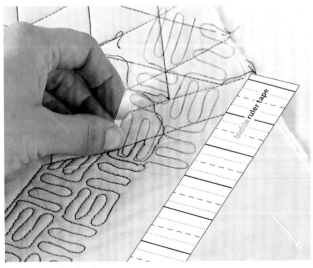
Pattern overlay for fragments

Butting Patterns

Mixing patterns is possible, and there is no rule I have ever heard of that says a quilted background can use only one pattern. You may be able to make some of these patterns transition from one into another, particularly if they use the same measurement for their basic grids—those with equilateral triangular grids come particularly to mind. However, if you have a definite mix of patterns and scale, I believe the patterns should have some sort of division between them. It can be as simple as a single or double line of stitching. I enjoy having a lot for the eye to look at on each of my quilts, and that includes having a variety of quilting patterns, if it is appropriate for the piece.

Compaction

Some of the patterns in this book have a lot more lines than others. Some have more open space. Most of them can be reduced or enlarged. The scale of quilting patterns can have great impact both visually and physically on a quilt. Of course, a small-scale pattern is going to be much more impressive than one with lots of space in between because of the amount of work. All the designs in this book are scalable—you just need to be able to do simple math to reduce them in size.

Compaction is my personal term for what happens to fabric and batting when it is quilted. My friend Georgia Bonesteel calls it "take up." The more quilting stitches in a quilt, the more it tends to shrink up, or compact. You can see that when there is dense quilting surrounding an unquilted area, the unquilted area tends to puff up and almost look like trapunto. Mixing different quilting patterns may cause problems, especially if they are quite different in scale or in the number of stitches that go into, say, a 3″ square.

I wish I were mathematical enough to figure out some sort of formula for compaction, but I tend to judge by eye, observing how many lines are in a pattern, how close together they are, and if overstitching

is involved. The Fractured Star pattern (page 70) is a good example of compaction. When I make the star pattern, the design is actually quite open. But when I change over to the repeat that makes a good border, the stitching is very dense and the sample is compacted a bit more on that side.

Why is compaction important? Because if a quilt is to lie flat, it should have a relatively consistent density over the whole surface. Most of my quilts are not quite flat when I am finished with them. Most of them get laundered in the washer and dryer (just until slightly damp) after they are complete. If the quilt is not flat after being washed, I iron it. A good blocking job can help with a quilt that doesn't have consistent compaction. There is an informative article on blocking at www.quiltuniversity.com/blocking.htm.

Leaving Spaces

Heavy and dense quilting is impressive. It seems that many top prizewinning quilts couldn't have another stitch put on them, they have been quilted so heavily. Not all quilts need to be quilted like that. Uh-oh, I may be editorializing a bit here. There is definitely such a thing as too little quilting, but can there not also be such a thing as too much quilting? Certainly a quilt that is to be actually used does not need closely packed quilting. Spaces can be left open, but if they are they should serve the purpose of the quilt's design. Spaces should not be left unquilted just because the minimum density the batting requires has been reached or it's too much work to come up with a quilting design for a space. I've seen many quilts in which the blocks have a sufficient amount of quilting, but the 2″ or 3″ sashing between the blocks is not quilted. It is an unattractive look—at least quilting ¼″ from the seams, down the sashing, would have provided a much more finished look.

In my art quilts, there are areas where I certainly do not want to put a lot of quilting—I want to allow the batting to puff the area out a bit, and additional lines of quilting could actually distract from the look I want to achieve.

In the end, you have to decide where it is appropriate to quilt and where not to quilt. It is you who most needs to be pleased with what you have created.

Finishing

STARTING AND STOPPING THE STITCHING

Method 1

Some quilters bring the threads to the top side of the quilt as they begin their stitching. This is done by letting the needle go down and up once through the quilt. Tug on the top thread, and a loop of the bobbin thread will appear. This can be done with the presser foot up or down.

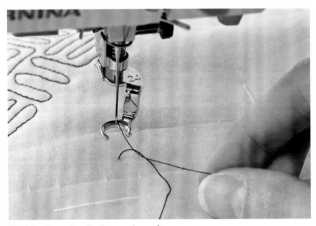

Pull up loop of bobbin thread.

Pull the bobbin thread to the top side of the quilt and then work with it as discussed below.

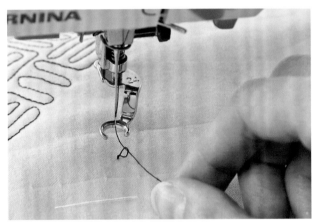

Bobbin thread pulled to quilt surface

Method 2

My machines have a feature that will knot the thread at the beginning and end of stitching by taking several stitches in the same place. I never use this feature—it leaves a big lump of thread on the back of the quilt that is very visible.

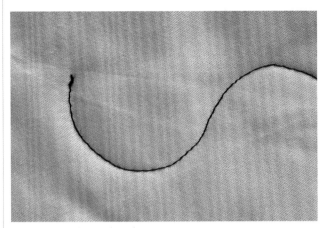

Lumps caused by machine knot

Method 3

Other quilters I know start and end with tiny stitches close together that probably hold tight and do not come out. This finish is hardly visible at all, but I still notice it. I would rather have the ends finished in a manner that is totally invisible.

Method 4

My preferred method is to start stitching and deal with the thread ends later.

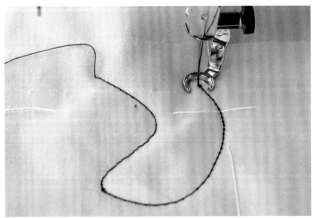

Stitching without pulling up bobbin thread

I do have some tangles on the back when I have done a lot of stitching and the bobbin threads get caught up in later rows. But somehow this seems easier to me than pulling the bobbin thread to the surface.

I tie knots—lots and lots of knots. It's kind of tedious work (I do it in front of the TV), but the beautifully finished ends are worth it to me. My favorite tool for tying in these thread ends is a self-threading or easy-threading needle. It has two eyes in the end. The lower one is like a regular needle that you have to poke the end of the thread through, but the upper eye has an opening in it between the two crests at the top.

Easy-threading needle

You can pull the side of the thread through this opening, and the upper eye is shaped so the thread does not pop back out through the opening. These needles are inexpensive and, within a package, some work better than others. Some will cut the thread rather than let it pop into the eye—throw these away. But there will also be some in the package that work fine.

To tie in the ends, insert the needle through the quilt into the base of the first (or last) stitch and pop the thread into the needle. Notice that there is a loop of thread.

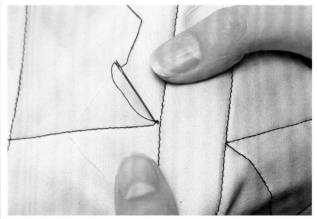

Insert easy-threading needle on top side of quilt.

If the thread is pulled up tightly against the needle, it may pop out of the eye before it pulls through, so bring the top thread through to the back side of the quilt.

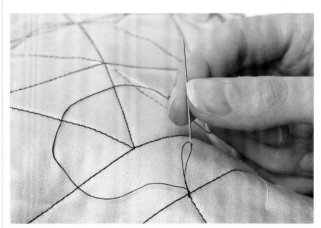

Pull thread through to back side.

Once both threads are on the back side of the quilt, tie a square knot. Remember, right over left and then left over right (or vice versa).

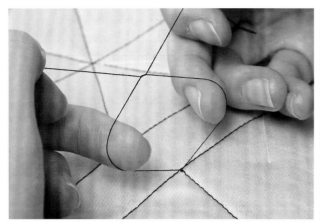

First half of square knot

The knot should be close to the base of the first (or last) stitch.

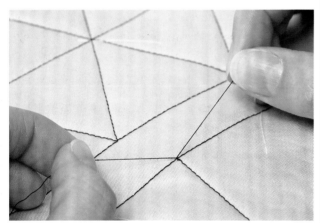

Knot is close to fabric.

Push the needle into the backing of the quilt and out about 1″ (or less) away. Take both thread ends and pop them into the easy-threading needle.

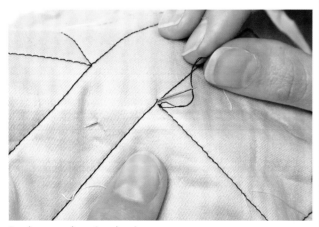

Ready to pop knot into batting

Pull the needle through, grab the threads, and give them a slight tug, which pops the knot through the backing and into the batting.

Point of needle shows where knot has disappeared.

Snip the remainder of the thread ends off at the surface of the quilt.

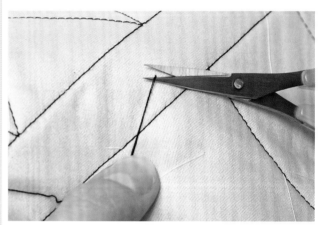

Cut off remaining thread.

The tidiness of this method gives a wonderful, consistent look. I suppose if I were to pull my bobbin threads to the top of the quilt I could use the same method to pop the knots in from the front. But every once in a while I have a knot that is very difficult and refuses to pop all the way inside the quilt. I would rather have this happen on the back side of the quilt than on the top.

Binding That Enhances

My mother taught me to finish the edges of quilts by turning the top and backing edges back and slip-stitching the edges together. Shortly after really getting into quilting, I made a quilt with this type of finished edge and had someone who had a lot more experience with quilts virtually turn her nose up at it. I've been putting binding on just about every quilt I've made since then. But lately when I've been judging, I've been seeing a lot more quilts that have been finished in this way without binding, and they seem appropriate.

I used to think that bias binding was the way to go, but lately I've also been making straight-grain binding and this works perfectly well, too. I had heard that certain members of the "quilt police" thought that all finished bindings should be ¼″ wide. I think a binding can be wider than that as long as it enhances, rather than draws attention from, the quilt as a whole.

Binding also reduces, by a large percentage, the number of thread ends I have to tie off. If I can begin or end on the edge of a quilt, no knots are needed because the thread ends are encased in the binding. I also think of a binding as a way to "frame" my quilt. Whereas a line going off the edge tends to keep the eye traveling, a line ending at a narrow binding can help contain the eye within the expanse of the quilt.

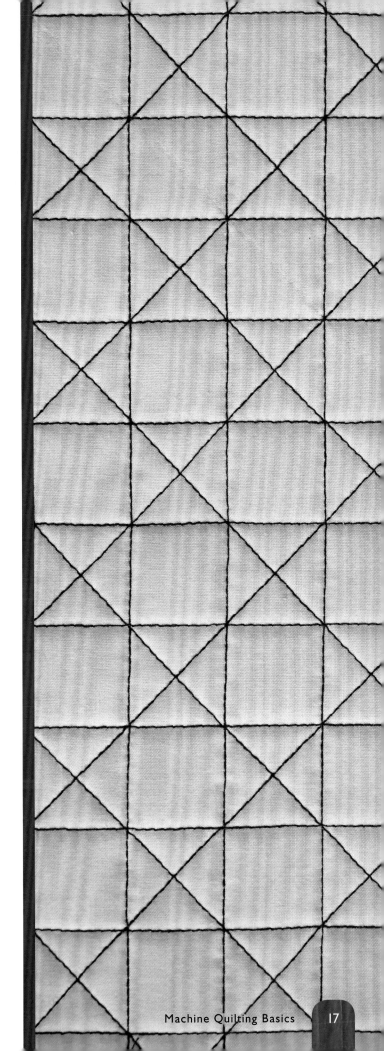

CHAPTER 2

Variations on V
V's and More V's

Right side up, upside down, or sideways, two diagonal lines that connect at one end make a V to me. Of course, you can say that a line going in one direction is a zig, and then when it makes a sharp corner it is a zag. If you put a whole line of V's together, they make a zigzag line. That is the premise behind many of the patterns in this book.

Here's one of the simple but effective patterns you can create with lots and lots of V's.

Herringbone

This design can give a very classy and interesting look to a quilt.

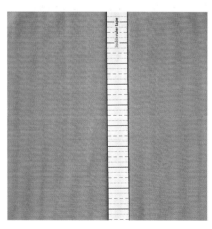

1. Make a vertical score line across the center of the sample. Stitch on the scored line.

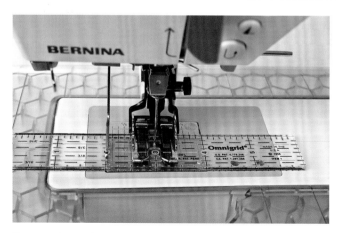

2. Use either Inchie Ruler Tape (C&T Publishing) or a sewing machine guide set to 1″ width.

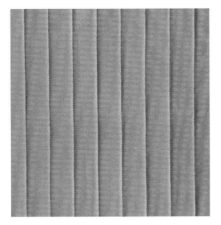

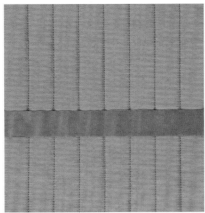

3. Stitch parallel lines, 1″ apart, to fill the space.

4. Make a horizontal score line across the center, perpendicular to the stitched lines. Place a length of 1″-wide masking tape with an edge on the score line.

5. Place 2 more lengths of masking tape, one on each side of the first piece.

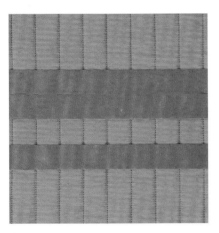

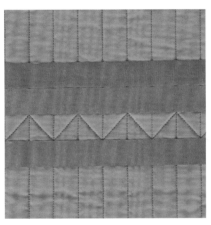

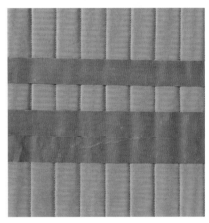

6. Remove the center piece of tape and place it on the outside edge of another piece of tape. The space revealed is your working area, and the stitched lines and pieces of tape create a row of squares. Moving the tape, which I call leapfrogging, is an easy way to place the next stitching line without any measuring or marking.

7. Starting at the first square on one end, stitch from a corner diagonally across the square to the other corner. Then, pivot and stitch across the second square in the opposite direction to form a wide V. Repeat for all the squares of the row.

8. Replace the original length of tape over the top of this row. Take another length of tape and place it on either side of the other 3 strips, so there are 4 strips; remove the piece next to the piece just placed to reveal a new row of squares.

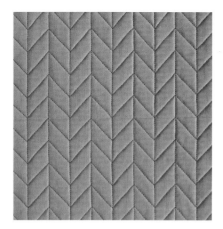

9. Stitch another row of V's that matches the first row. Keep moving the lengths of tape across the area and stitching in both directions until the area is filled with rows of V's and creates a herringbone pattern.

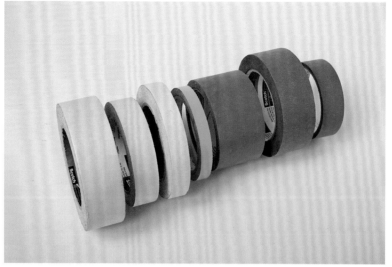

This pattern can be varied in many ways by changing the width of the parallel rows and the width of the masking tape. I have almost a dozen different widths of masking tape, and every time I think a package I'm looking at might be a bit different, I buy it.

Even if the tape says on the package that it is 1″ wide, it may not be. In fact, most of the less expensive brands are ⅛″ narrower than the stated width. Most manufacturers make their tape in the metric equivalent nearest our standard 1″, 2″, and so on. So, be aware.

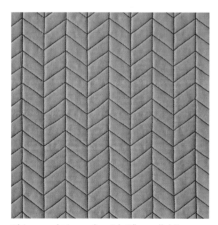

This sample is made with 1″ parallel lines and ½″-wide tape, creating shallow V's.

This sample is made with 1″ parallel lines and 1½″-wide tape, creating deeper V's.

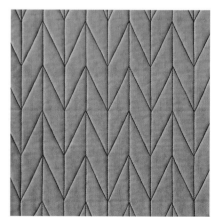

This sample is made with 1″ parallel lines and 2″-wide tape, creating extremely deep V's.

Another variation can be created by using 2 different widths of masking tape. Try your own variations by changing the widths of the original parallel lines and mixing up the sizes of tape. This pattern has a hint of dimensionality to it and looks like pleated stripes.

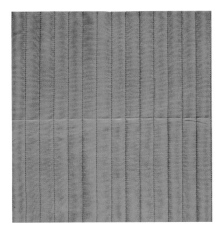

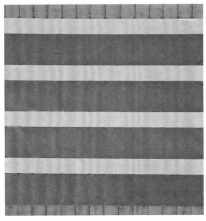

1. Use ¾"-wide masking tape and fill the sample with parallel rows of stitching. Then make a horizontal score line across the center, perpendicular to the stitched lines.

2. Place a strip of ¾" tape next to the score line, and then add 2 strips of 1½"-wide tape, 1 on each side of the ¾" strip. Continue alternating the strips until the area is filled.

3. Remove the narrower tape strips and stitch rows of V's between them.

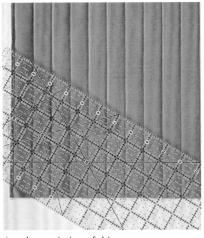

Another variation of this pattern uses a change in the angle of the second scored line.

1. Instead of using a perpendicular line, score a 60° angle using the proper line on a ruler.

2. Place a length of masking tape with an edge on the score line. Then, place the lengths of tape as for Herringbone, Step 5 (page 19).

3. Remove the center piece of tape to reveal a row of 60° diamonds. Stitch irregular V's down this row—the first line of the V goes the length of the diamond and the second half of the V goes the width of the diamond.

4. Continue placing the tape and stitching to create a slanted herringbone.

CHAPTER 3

Patterns Using
Inchie Ruler Tape

inchie ruler tape

Easy, Accurate Guide for Quilting, Crafting, Painting & More

- Handy, repositionable adhesive strips marked in ¼" increments for easy measuring
- Just peel and stick for perfect alignment of:
  - Machine-quilting designs
  - Embroidery
  - Hand-quilting stitches
  - Beadwork
  - Papercrafting elements
  - Stencils
  - Faux painting patterns
- Safe to use on fabric

Inspired by Charlotte Warr Andersen's Innovative Book, One Line at a Time!

C&T PUBLISHING

80 1" × 11" peel-off paper rulers

©2009 C&T Publishing ©2009 C&T Publishing ©2009 C&T Publishing ©2009 C&T Publishing
www.ctpub.com www.ctpub.com www.ctpub.com www.ctpub.com

When I first started this technique of stitching patterns, one line at a time and without marking, I used 1"-wide masking tape that I had laid out on a cutting mat and marked every inch. After I submitted the manuscript for *One Line at a Time*, the good folks at C&T Publishing came up with the brilliant idea of Inchie Ruler Tape. I started using it and after going through a few packages found that I'd much rather use the Inchie Ruler Tape than take the time to make marked masking tape. I have also found that it can be used multiple times, and it has really increased the range of patterns I can make.

I use the heck out of my Inchie Ruler Tape. I use it until it will no longer cling to the fabric. I can get quite large areas of quilting done using just 3 or 4 pieces. I stick them end to end when I'm doing large areas. I peel them up slowly and carefully rather than pulling them off quickly, because they do rip if they've been snagged with stitching. I don't give up on one if I've ripped it and it's still sticky; I put it back together with clear tape, matching up the markings. A package of Inchie Ruler Tape can really be made to last.

Of course, if you're still reluctant to use it, you can take the time to create your own using 1"-wide masking tape and a fine black marker.

Serpentine Zigzag I

Here is a very simple but effective pattern—it's easy to create, and it works great as a fill or border.

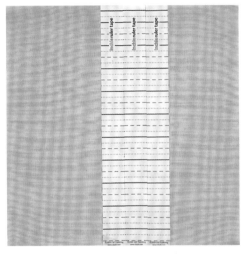

1. Make a vertical score line across the center of the sample. Place a piece of Inchie Ruler Tape with an edge on the score line. Then, add a piece of tape on each side, aligning the inch marks.

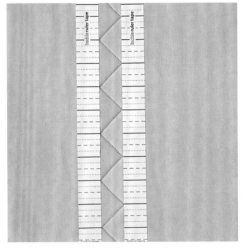

2. Remove the middle piece of tape and stitch a zigzag line from 1″ mark to 1″ mark.

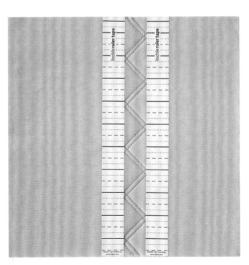

3. Now stitch a zigzag line from ¾″ mark to ¾″ mark, creating a staggered echo of the first row.

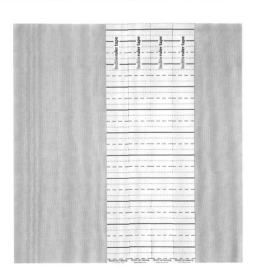

4. Replace the middle piece of tape, and then add a fourth piece to the smaller area of the sample.

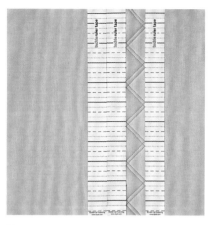

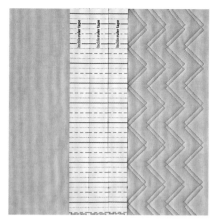

5. Remove the piece of tape next to the piece that was just added and stitch 2 rows of staggered zigzags just like the first set.

6. Continue stitching rows of staggered zigzags until half the area has been filled. One of the original pieces of tape will be left on the unstitched area.

7. Place a piece of tape on each side of this remaining piece.

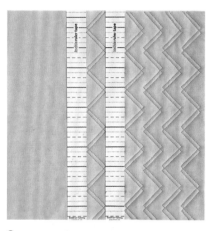

If you don't need a centered design, there is nothing wrong with starting from one side and filling a whole area with this pattern going in one direction. Just make sure that the zigzag rows are stacked.

8. Remove the middle piece. Now, stitch rows that are the mirror image of the first set of rows.

9. Continue to fill the remaining half of the area with these mirror-image rows.

Valley Sunrise by Georgia Bonesteel

A quilt with a definite "glow," this work features the Serpentine Zigzag pattern. The quilting design complements the scene and looks like heat and warmth rising from the valley.

Serpentine Zigzag II

An abstract quilt would look great with this architectural and angular design.

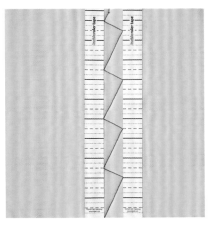

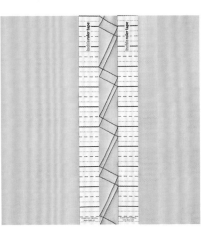

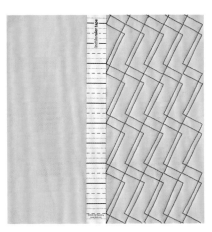

1. Make a vertical score line across the center of the sample. Place a piece of Inchie Ruler Tape with an edge on the score line. Add a piece of tape on each side, aligning the inch marks.

2. Remove the middle piece of tape. Starting on the upper right, stitch left diagonally across 2″ and then right diagonally ½″. Repeat to create a zigzag line.

3. Stitch a second zigzag line starting on the upper left and stitching right diagonally across ½″ and then left diagonally across 2″. Repeat to create an asymmetrical pattern.

4. Replace the middle piece of tape, and then add a fourth piece of tape to the smaller area of the sample. Remove the piece next to the piece that was just added and stitch the 2 rows of the lopsided, staggered zigzag just like the first. Continue stitching these rows until the right half of the area has been filled. Notice that the corners of these rows connect. One of the original pieces of tape will be left on the unstitched area.

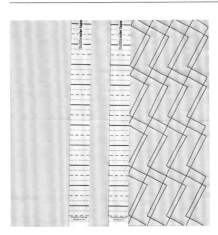

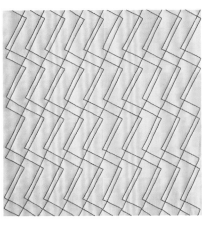

5. Place a piece of tape on each side of the remaining piece. Remove the middle piece. Stitch zigzag rows as instructed above, working to the left.

6. This finished design has movement and eye appeal.

Note:

The first row is in red and the second in blue.

Double Kites

This design looks like double images of tessellating kites. The key to success with this pattern is care in making sure the corners of the zigzag match from row to row.

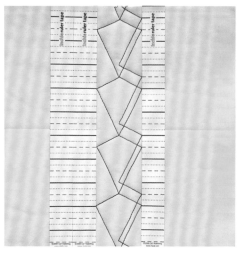

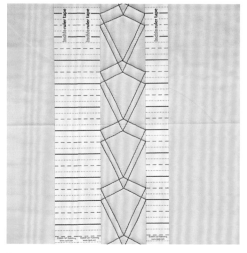

1. Follow Steps 1–3 for Serpentine Zigzag II (page 25), stitching a row of zigzags as instructed. Place the third piece of tape to the left.

2. Peel up the piece of tape on the right side of the zigzag just worked and place it on the outside left. Stitch a mirror image of the first row using the corners of the first row of zigzag on one side and the Inchie Ruler Tape on the other side.

3. Stitch a mirror image of the second row using the corners of the first row of zigzag on one side and the Inchie Ruler Tape on the other side to create double kite shapes.

4. Working outward from the center, stitch alternating rows of lopsided, staggered zigzag to fill the area.

Darts

Here's a pattern that's extremely easy to do yet looks complex—tessellating darts are created to make this eye-catching pattern.

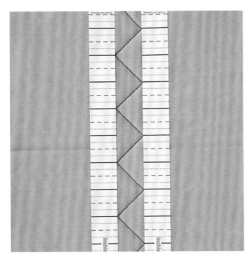

1. Make vertical and horizontal score lines across the center of the sample. Place a piece of Inchie Ruler Tape with an edge on the vertical score line. Add a piece of tape on each side of the first piece, aligning the inch marks. Remove the middle piece. Starting at an inch mark at one end, stitch a zigzag line from inch mark to inch mark.

2. Leapfrog the tape and fill the sample with rows of zigzag right next to each other, all going the same direction. Align the inch marks of the tape to keep the work centered.

3. Starting at the top of a row of zigzag (blue), stitch another row of zigzag (red) from point to point.

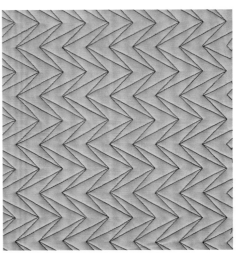

4. Repeat Step 3 to stitch sharper angled rows of zigzag within the other rows.

Rolling X

I named this pattern "Rolling X" because the shape looks like it could roll in one direction.

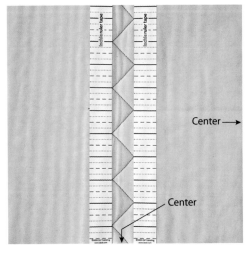

1. Make vertical and horizontal lines ½" off the center of the sample. Place a piece of Inchie Ruler Tape with an edge on the vertical score line to make the tape lie exactly in the middle of the sample. Make sure an inch mark is on the horizontal score line. Then, add a piece of tape on each side, aligning the inch marks. Remove the middle piece of tape. Starting at an inch mark at one end, stitch a zigzag line diagonally from inch mark to inch mark.

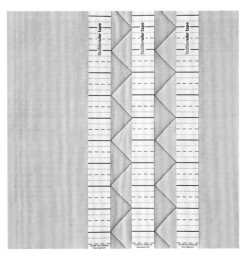

2. Add 2 more pieces of tape to one side. Remove the middle of the 3 pieces of tape that are together. Stitch another row of zigzag.

3. Leapfrog the tape to fill the sample with rows of zigzag spaced 1" apart, all going the same direction.

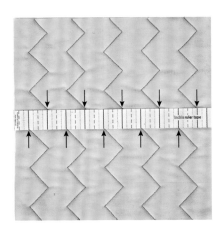

4. Place a piece of tape on the horizontal score line, with every other inch mark aligned on the points of the rows of zigzag stitching. On the other edge of the tape, every other inch mark should also be touching zigzag points.

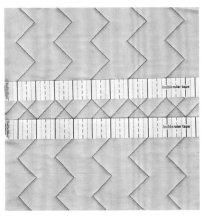

5. Add a piece of tape on each side, aligning the inch marks, so there are 3 pieces of tape, and then remove the middle piece. Starting at an inch mark at one end, stitch diagonally from inch mark to inch mark. An X should be formed only when one direction of the zigzag is stitched.

6. Repeat, stitching horizontal zigzag rows, skipping every other inch. Make sure the inch marks on the tape match (or come close to matching) the points of the zigzag.

This pattern can be taken a little further, however.

Paving Stones I

This pattern looks like double bricks that form a square, and these squares alternate directions like some paving stones do.

It seems a shame to mess up a pattern as nice as Rolling X with another pattern that actually looks simpler. But these paving stones need the structure of the Rolling X to be constructed.

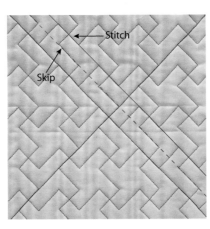

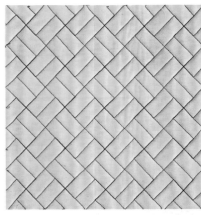

1. Complete Steps 1–6 of the Rolling X pattern (page 28). Stitch a diagonal line from corner to corner in both directions, keeping the overstitching as on line as possible.

2. If you look closely, there is another series of diagonal lines about ⅝″ away that could be connected—skip these and go to the next series of diagonal lines.

3. Stitch on the next series of diagonal lines in both directions, keeping the overstitching as on line as possible.

CHAPTER 4

More Patterns Using Inchie Ruler Tape
Diamonds

Although the patterns discussed in this chapter are created by sewing simple zigzags, somewhat stricter attention needs to be paid to the placement of the rows. So marking the Inchie Ruler Tape can be helpful.

Diamond Columns

Chains of end-to-end diamonds are easily created in this pattern.

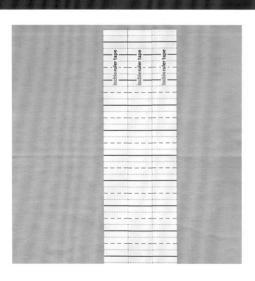

1. Make vertical and horizontal score lines across the center of the sample. Place a piece of Inchie Ruler Tape with an edge on the vertical score line. Make sure an inch mark is on the horizontal score line. Then, add a piece of tape on each side, aligning the inch marks.

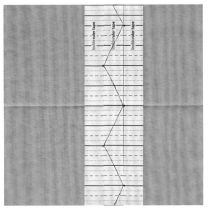

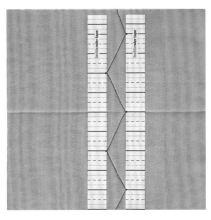

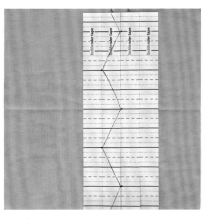

2. Start at the horizontal score line and draw a zigzag line diagonally across 2″ back and forth on the middle piece of tape. Put dots on the inside edges of both outside pieces of tape to show the corners for stitching.

3. Remove the middle piece of tape and stitch the zigzag line from dot to dot.

4. Replace the marked zigzag piece of tape over the stitching. Add a fourth piece of tape to the side with the smaller area.

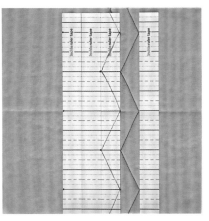

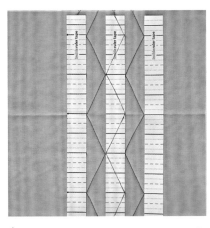

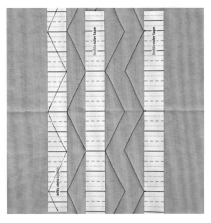

5. Remove the dotted piece of tape on the right that is between the new piece and the marked zigzag tape, and place it next to the other dotted piece of tape. Stitch a zigzag line that echoes the first row.

6. Remove the middle of the 3 pieces of tape that are together and stitch a zigzag line that is a mirror image of the first 2 rows to create large diamonds.

7. Move the zigzag marked tape next to the dotted tape on the left. Place a piece of tape over the stitching from Step 6. Remove the middle of the 3 pieces of tape that are together and add a row of stitching that echoes the third row.

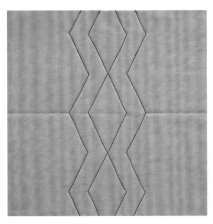

9. Continue placing the pieces of tape and stitching until the space is filled.

8. The first 4 rows of stitching form echoed diamonds.

Double X

1. Create the Diamond Columns pattern as previously instructed. Place a piece of Inchie Ruler Tape with an edge on the horizontal score line. Make sure an inch mark is on the vertical score line. Then, add a piece of tape on each side, aligning the inch marks. Draw a zigzag so a corner is on the center of the piece (the center of the diamond in the middle). This center placement is very important, and the pattern will not turn out right if this dot is not in the center. Add dots to the outer pieces of tape.

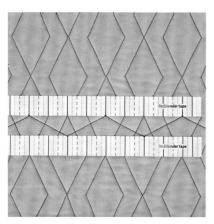

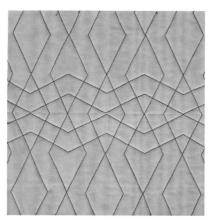

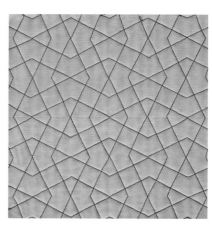

2. Remove the middle piece of tape and stitch the zigzag line from dot to dot.

3. Repeat Steps 4–7 for Diamond Columns (page 31) to make the first 4 rows of stitching (blue).

4. Repeat these 4 rows to fill the space.

Intertwined Stars

This pattern looks awesomely complicated but is created with just lopsided zigzag and overstitching.

1. Make vertical and horizontal score lines that are ½" off the center. Place a piece of Inchie Ruler Tape along the edge of the vertical score line. Make sure an inch mark is on the horizontal score line. Then, add a piece of tape on each side, aligning the inch marks. Draw a zigzag on the middle piece of tape. Start by finding the center, which should be ½" above or below the score line on the middle piece of tape, and mark a dot. Mark diagonally across 3" with the dot in the center. Mark diagonally across 1", then 3". Notice that on the edges you run out of tape, so you have to guess or actually measure the angle for that next 3" gap.

Using a different color of pencil, make dots on the outside pieces of tape to show where the corners are.

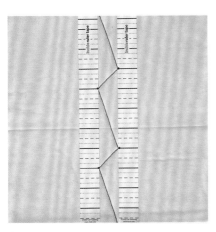

2. Remove the middle piece of tape and stitch from dot to dot to make the zigzag.

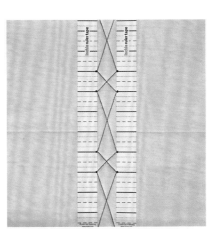

3. Stitch the mirror image to create elongated kite shapes.

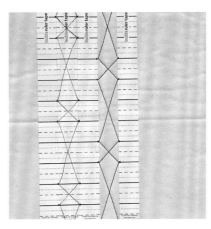

4. Place 2 pieces of tape to the left of a remaining piece. The zigzag needs to be staggered for this next row. Mark diagonally across 3" and 1", but opposite to the first stitching. Make marks on the outside pieces of tape to show the corners.

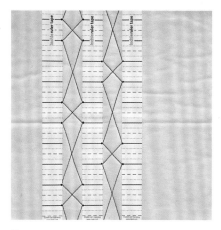

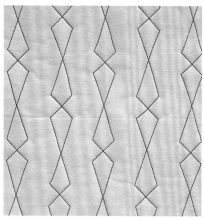

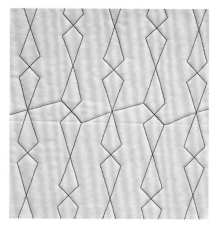

5. Remove the middle piece of tape. Stitch from corner to corner to create a staggered version of the first row of stitching.

6. Complete the staggered rows, spaced 1″ apart, across the sample.

7. Rotate the piece and stitch through an intersection to the first corner, then overstitch across a leg of the short X, then stitch across the center of the elongated X, and then overstitch again. Repeat across.

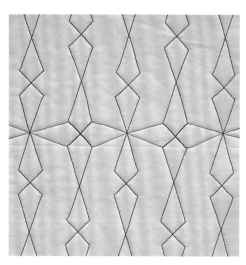

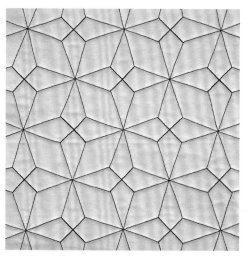

8. Stitch a mirror image of the row just completed to make elongated kite shapes going in opposite directions.

9. Make opposing rows every other inch to fill the space.

Diamond Plaid

This pattern has a very starry look to it but is created with only zigzag rows.

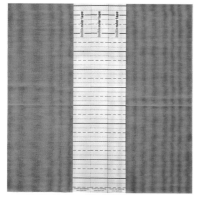

1. Make a vertical score line that is ½″ off the center. Make a horizontal score line across the center. Place a piece of Inchie Ruler Tape along the edge of the vertical score line. Make sure a half-inch mark is on the horizontal score line. This tape should now be exactly in the center of the sample. Add a piece of tape on each side, aligning the inch marks.

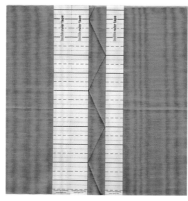

2. Remove the middle piece of tape and place it next to the outside left piece. Stitch diagonally across 2″ from inch mark to inch mark to make a zigzag.

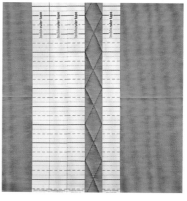

3. Stitch a mirror-image row of zigzags to create a row of diamonds. Add a piece of tape next to the outside left piece.

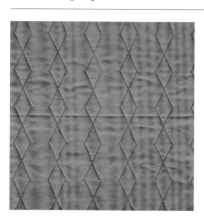

4. Remove the middle of the 3 pieces of tape that are together and sew a row of diamonds. Continue using 3 pieces of tape to space the rows and removing the middle of the 3 to create rows of diamonds vertically across the sample. Each row of diamonds is separated by 1″.

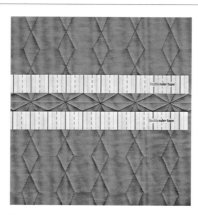

5. Place a piece of tape along the horizontal score line, aligning the inch marks on the tape with the intersection of the X underneath. Add a piece of tape on each side, aligning the inch marks. When you peel up the middle piece of tape, you should see nice, symmetrical X's.

6. Stitch diagonally across 2″ from inch mark to inch mark to create diamonds, with the stitching line going through the middle of the X's (red).

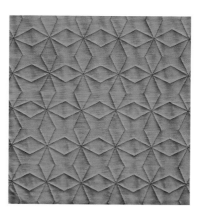

7. Continue placing the pieces of tape and stitching rows of diamonds to fill the space.

CHAPTER 5

Even More Patterns Using Inchie Ruler Tape
Zippers

Unlike the designs presented in the previous two chapters, which used zigzag stitching lines, the patterns in this chapter use what I call a "zipper" line because it's like the teeth of zippers that are meshed together.

Wonky Bow Ties

This pattern will look something like bow ties that have gone askew.

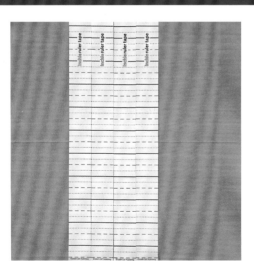

1. Make a vertical score line across the center of the sample. Place a piece of Inchie Ruler Tape with the left edge on the score line. Add 3 more pieces of tape to the left side, aligning the inch marks.

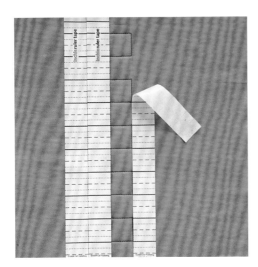

2. Remove 1 of the middle pieces of tape. Stitch down to the first inch mark on the left-side piece of tape. Pivot and stitch directly across the work area to the corresponding inch mark on the right-side piece of tape. Pivot and stitch to the next inch mark along the edge of the tape. Pivot and stitch directly across the work area to the corresponding inch mark on the right-side piece of tape and pivot. Repeat to the bottom of the sample, creating a "zipper" line.

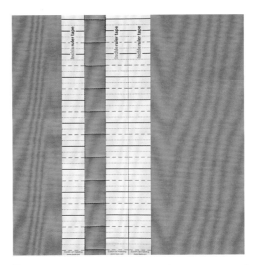

3. Replace the piece of tape on the area just stitched. Remove the piece of tape to its left. Stitch down to the first half-inch mark on the left-side piece of tape. Pivot and stitch directly across the work area to the corresponding half-inch mark on the right-side piece of tape. Pivot and stitch to the next half-inch mark along the edge of the tape. Pivot and stitch directly across the work area to the corresponding half-inch mark on the left-side piece of tape and pivot. Repeat to the bottom of the sample.

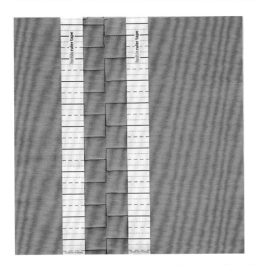

4. Remove the tape covering the first row of stitching.

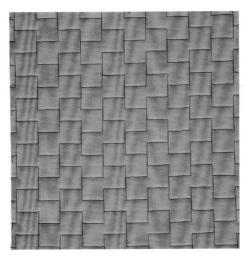

5. Continue placing and moving the pieces of tape to stitch alternating rows of "zippers" that are sewn on the inch marks and then the half-inch marks.

Twin Squares

Here's a variation on the "zipper" pattern that is symmetrical but with a slightly random look.

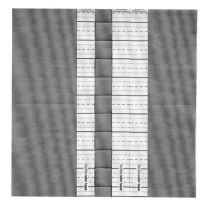

1. Make a vertical score line ½" off center and a horizontal score line across the center. Place an edge of the Inchie Ruler Tape on the vertical score line. Make sure a half-inch mark is on the horizontal score line. Complete a row of the "zipper" line following Steps 1 and 2 for Wonky Bow Ties (page 36). This row should be exactly in the center of the sample.

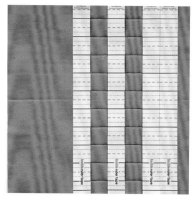

2. Position another piece of tape, so there are 3 together; then remove the middle piece and place it next to the right piece to create a new working area. Stitch a row of the zipper line just like the first.

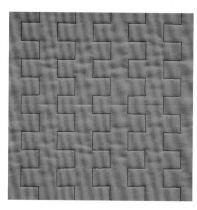

3. Continue stitching rows until the area is filled with vertical zipper rows, all going in the same direction. Keep track of which edge is the top of the sample.

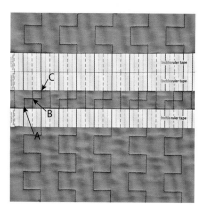

4. Place a piece of tape above the horizontal score line, then another piece on each side of the first. Remove the middle piece of tape and place it next to an outside piece. Stitch to the first half-inch mark on the left-side piece of tape and pivot; then stitch directly across the work area to the corresponding half-inch mark on the right-side piece of tape and pivot.

Stitch to the next half-inch mark along the edge of the tape. Pivot and then stitch across the previous stitching to the corresponding half-inch mark on the left-side piece of tape and pivot. Repeat down the work area. You will be crossing previous stitching when stitching along the edge of the tape (A, C) and every other time you cross the work area (B).

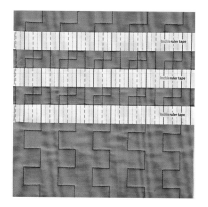

5. Add a fourth piece of tape to create a group of 3. Remove the middle piece and stitch another row of horizontal zipper.

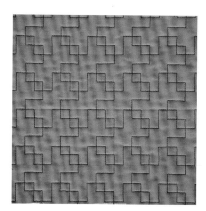

6. Continue stitching horizontal zipper rows every other inch across the area to create the Twin Squares pattern.

Cartwheels

This intricate-looking pattern involves the very same stitching that is done to make Twin Squares (page 38), but the horizontal rows in this pattern are the mirror image of the rows in that pattern.

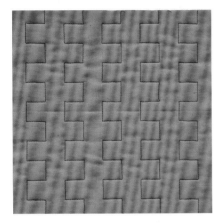

1. Stitch the vertical rows of "zippers" following Steps 1–3 for Twin Squares (page 38).

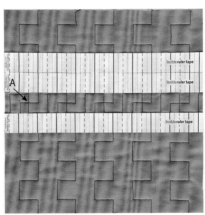

2. Place a piece of tape above the horizontal score line, then another piece on each side of the first. Remove the middle piece of tape and place it next to an outside piece. Stitch to the first half-inch mark on the right-side piece of tape and pivot; then stitch directly across the work area to the corresponding half-inch mark on the left-side piece of tape and pivot. Stitch to the next half-inch mark along the edge of the tape. Pivot and then stitch across the previous stitching to the corresponding half-inch mark on the right-side piece of tape and pivot. Each previous row of zipper should only be stitched across once. Repeat down the work area. Notice the subtle change in this pattern: the stitching begins on the opposite side of the work area and the previous stitching is only crossed once on each "tooth" (A).

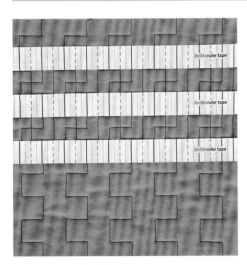

3. Add a fourth piece of tape to create a group of 3. Remove the middle piece and stitch another row of horizontal zipper.

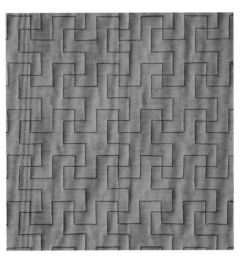

4. Continue stitching horizontal zipper rows every other inch across the area. The resulting pattern reminds me of the cartwheels I used to be able to do when I was much younger.

CHAPTER 6

Squares + Diamonds

This pattern looks tricky but is actually quite simple to create with the aid of templates.

The alternating squares and diamonds form rows, and the rows are mirror images. To differentiate between the two types of rows, one template is pink and yellow and the other is blue and lime green.

The 60° diamond pattern gives a more subtle texture, while the 45° template looks more dimensional.

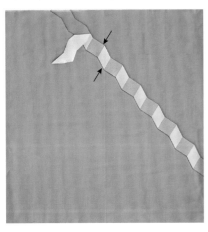

1. Make a vertical score line through the center of the sample.

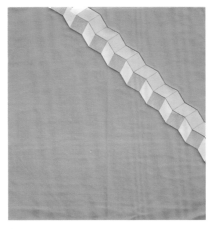

2. See Pattern Templates (page 11) for guidance in making the Squares & Diamonds templates (page 42). Cut out a pink and yellow template from the label paper. Place it so one end goes off the sample and a diamond shape has its sharp points on the scored line. Stitch on both sides of the template, pivoting at the corners.

3. Cut out a green and blue template from the label paper. Fit it tightly next to the pink and yellow template and stitch along the open side.

4. Cut out another green and blue template and place it along the opposite side of the pink and yellow template. Stitch along the open side of this strip. Then carefully peel up the pink and yellow strip and leapfrog it over the second blue and green strip, matching up the corners. Stitch along the open edge of the pink and yellow strip.

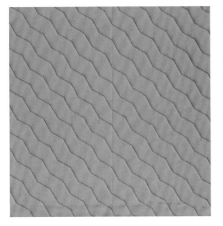

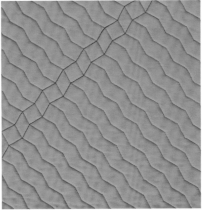

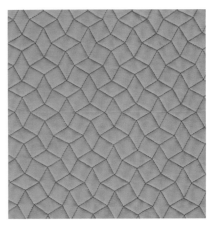

5. Continue alternating the templates across the sample until there are zigzag diagonal lines all the way across it.

6. Now, stitch in the opposite direction, connecting the corners to make squares and diamonds. Look for parallel lines in the zigzag that will make up a square; then the next part of the zigzag will make a diamond when the lines are joined from corner to corner. You can use a template strip to get started, but after establishing a line you should be able to complete the diagonals by just stitching from corner to corner.

7. The completed pattern is entertaining to the eye and makes a great background for feathers and other motifs.

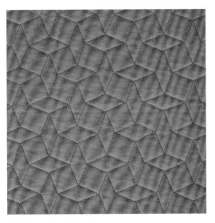

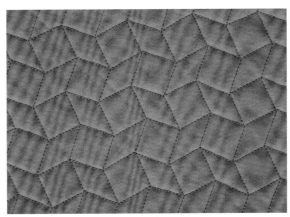

The Squares & Diamonds template pattern—45° (page 43) uses 45° diamonds and is larger in scale. The corners are also more pronounced; therefore it is easier to use. It gives a slightly different perspective from the one with the 60° diamonds.

If the template is used vertically rather than diagonally, the look is quite different.

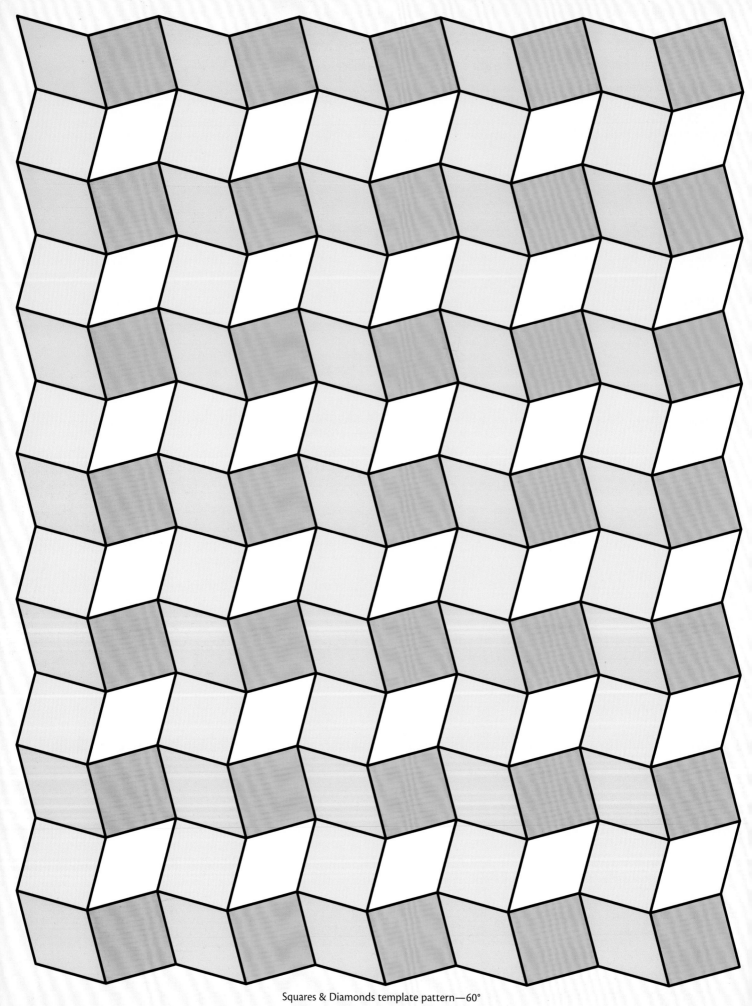

Squares & Diamonds template pattern—60°

Squares & Diamonds template pattern—45°

CHAPTER 7

Enhancing a Grid

A grid can be made in any size you want, but 1″ is a nice working size. It's a boring pattern all by itself, but we can do several things over the top of it to make it more exciting.

Paving Stones II

This pattern is something I spotted in a combat photo from Afghanistan. The stones on the ground in the photo were laid in this manner.

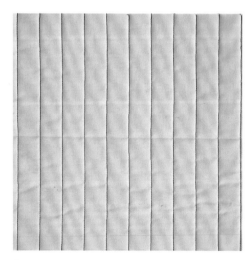

1. Follow Steps 1–3 for Herringbone (page 18) to stitch 1″ parallel lines.

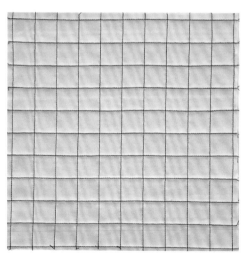

2. Rotate the sample and repeat to stitch 1″ parallel lines perpendicular to the first lines to create a 1″ grid.

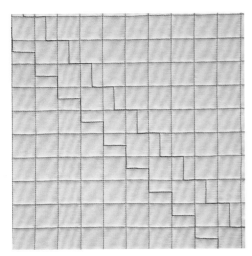

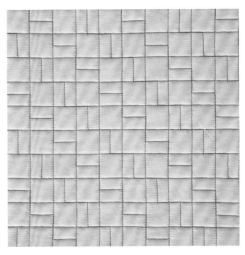

3. Start at an edge and overstitch down a grid line until the midpoint of the first square is reached. (You can mark where the midpoints are, count stitches, or, my favorite way, just eyeball it.) Then pivot and stitch through the middle of the square, dividing it in half; pivot and overstitch to the midpoint of the square on the next row. Repeat this zigzag diagonally across the grid. Skip a diagonal row of squares and make the next diagonal row of zigzag in mirror image to the first row. The stitching is shown in red for illustration purposes.

4. Repeat the diagonal rows of zigzag on every other row, making each a mirror image of the row just completed.

Broken Dishes

The name for this pattern comes from a traditional quilt block, and the pattern is very easy to create.

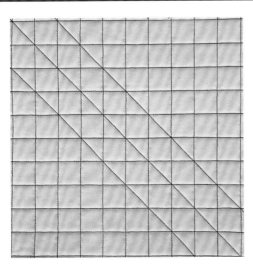

1. Follow Steps 1 and 2 for Paving Stones II (page 44) to create a 1″ grid.

2. Stitch straight diagonal lines through the middle of every other diagonal row of squares, dividing the squares in half. (This stitching is shown in red for illustration purposes.) Fill the grid with these diagonal lines in one direction.

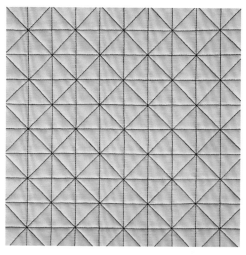

3. Now stitch straight diagonal lines through the middle of every other diagonal row of squares in the opposite direction, so the remaining squares are divided in half.

4. Fill the remaining rows to divide all the squares into half-square triangles. The resulting pattern will resemble the traditional Broken Dishes pattern.

Ohio Star

This pattern is created using the same lines and same amount of stitching as Broken Dishes (page 45).

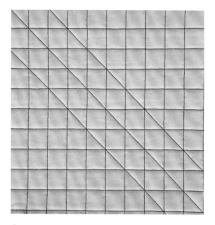

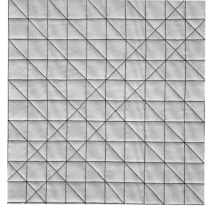

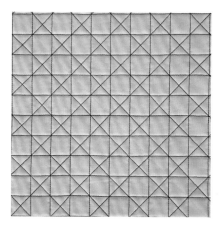

1. Follow Steps 1 and 2 for Paving Stones II (page 44) to create a 1″ grid.

2. Stitch straight diagonal lines through the middle of every other diagonal row of squares, dividing the squares into triangles. Fill the space with these diagonal lines in one direction. (This stitching is shown in red for illustration purposes.)

3. Stitch diagonally in the opposite direction through the squares that have been divided into triangles so that there are now 4 triangles in each of these squares.

4. Fill the remaining rows, and the resulting pattern will resemble the traditional Ohio Star pattern.

Structured Clamshell Leaves

This pattern is made using the Clamshell template (page 48). To use it for the patterns in this chapter, the sewn grid will need to be precisely 1″. To use a larger or smaller grid, the template needs to be enlarged or reduced to fit the length of two squares of the grid.

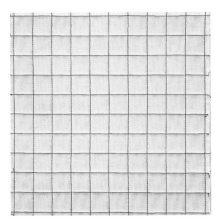

1. Follow Steps 1 and 2 for Paving Stones II (page 44) to create a 1″ grid.

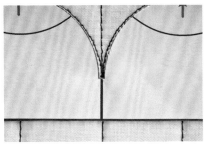

2. Copy the Clamshell pattern (page 48) onto a full sheet of label paper. See Pattern Templates (page 11) for guidance in making the pattern templates. Then, cut out a template on the red line, which should still show on the edge of the template after being cut. Be sure to cut out the small square notch at the bottom of each arc to give the sewing machine needle room to sew.

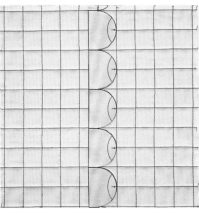

3. Place the arrows of the Clamshell template on the intersections of a row of the grid. The notches of the template should meet the intersections on the next row over. Stitch along the edge of the template with a free-motion foot and the feed dogs down.

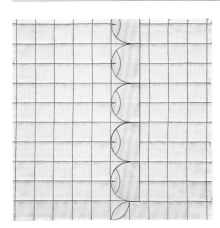

4. Turn the template to face the opposite direction, move the template over a square, and stitch to form a leaf shape in each square of the row.

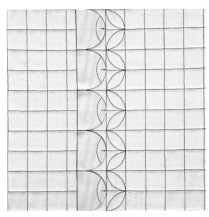

5. Position the template on another row as in Step 3 and stitch.

6. Reposition the template as in Step 4 and stitch. Repeat these steps to achieve rows of undulating leaves.

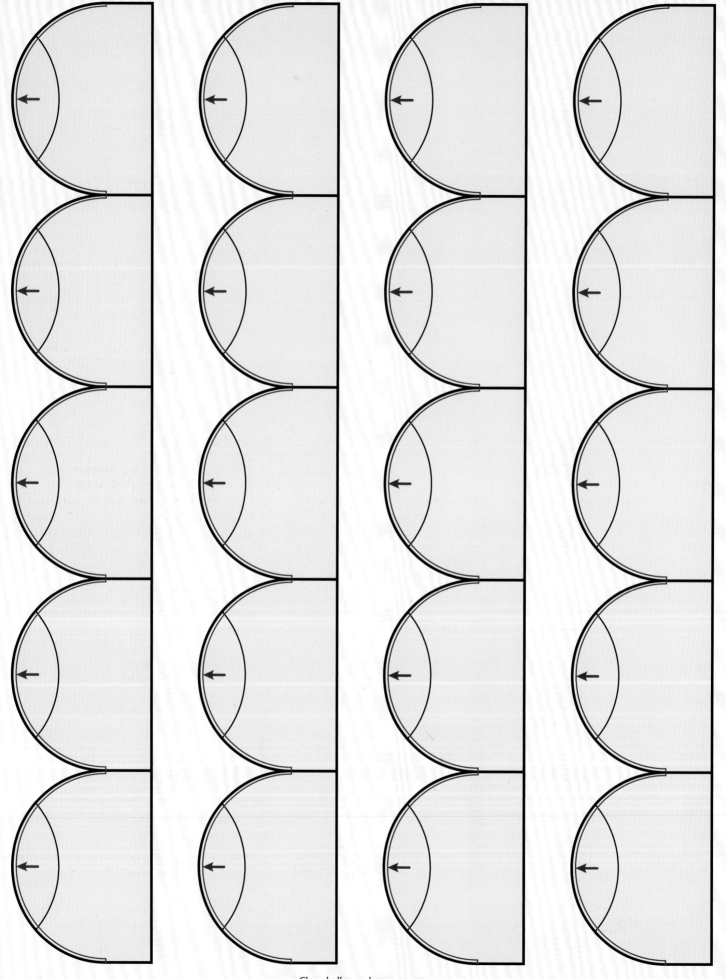

Clamshell template pattern

Structured Orange Peel

This pattern is stitched just like the Structured Clamshell Leaves (page 47), but the rows alternate in direction.

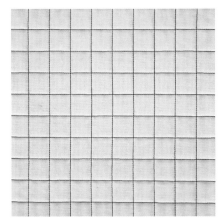

1. Follow Steps 1 and 2 for Paving Stones II (page 44) to create a 1″ grid and Step 2 of Structured Clamshell Leaves (page 47) to make the template.

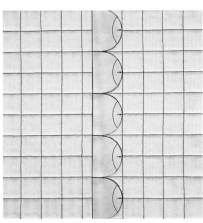

2. Place the arrows of the Clamshell template on the intersections of a row of the grid. The notches of the template should meet the intersections on the next row over. Stitch along the edge of the template with a free-motion foot and the feed dogs down.

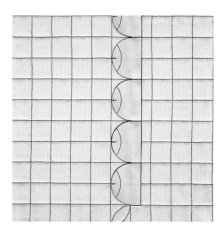

3. Turn the template to face the opposite direction, move the template over a square, and stitch to form a leaf shape in each square of the row.

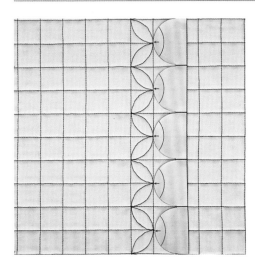

4. Repeat Steps 2 and 3, placing the Clamshell template to create a mirror image of the first stitching.

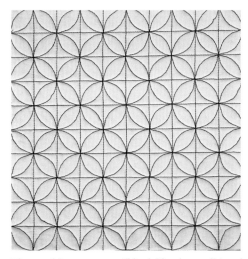

The resulting pattern will look like the traditional Orange Peel pattern imposed over a grid.

Structured Squiggles

This pattern is fun to do since it doesn't require perfect free-motion quilting.

1. Follow Steps 1 and 2 for Paving Stones II (page 44) to create a 1″ grid.

2. Stitch the motif in each square of a diagonal row with a free-motion foot and the feed dogs down.

3. Skip a diagonal row of squares and stitch another diagonal row of squiggles. Continue this step until the piece has been filled. You can stop here and use this as the completed design or continue.

4. Now, work diagonally in the other direction. Fill the remaining empty squares with the same squiggle stitched in rows (red).

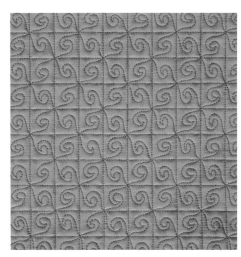

The resulting pattern looks awesomely complicated, but you know the secret of creating it.

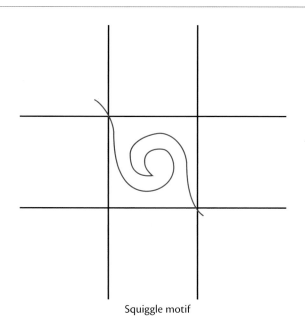

Squiggle motif

Structured Doodle Weave

This is a playful and fun design that will help hone your free-motion skills.

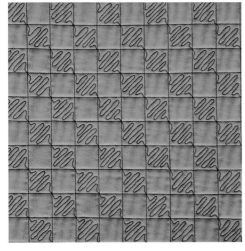

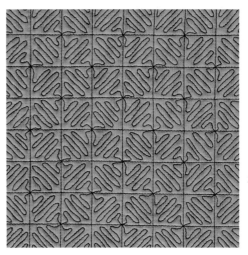

1. Using the same sequence as the previous pattern, change the motif to a back-and-forth doodle motif. Fill the squares in every other diagonal row. This is a very attractive design by itself.

2. Stitch rows of doodles in the opposite direction to give the resulting pattern a woven look.

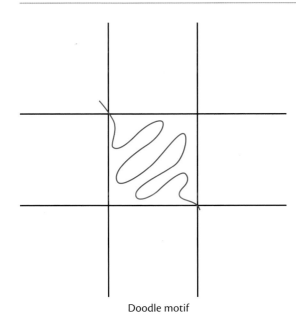

Doodle motif

CHAPTER 8

Template Patterns

The Clamshell template is much more versatile than I originally thought it to be, and there are many variations that won't have you instantly thinking "clamshell," as evidenced by the patterns in the previous chapter. But I have several more.

Linked Leaves

This would be a good pattern for a narrow border.

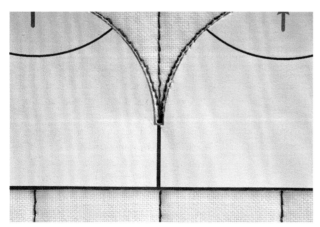

1. Follow Step 2 of Structured Clamshell Leaves (page 47) to make the template.

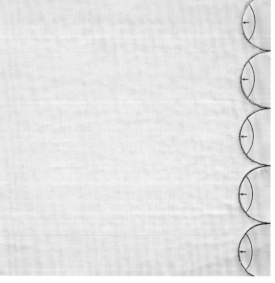

2. Position the straight base of the template on an edge of the sample. Stitch along the scalloped edge of the template with a free-motion foot and the feed dogs down.

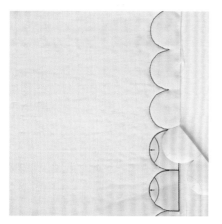 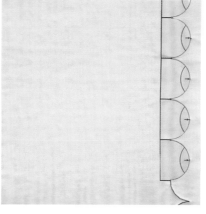 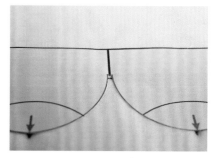

3. Remove the template.

4. Rotate the template and place it so the arrows are on the points of the stitching and the barest amount of thread from the tops of the half-circles can be seen in the notches of the template.

This sideways close-up may show this a little better. Stitch along the edge of the template.

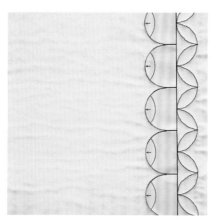 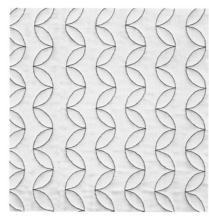 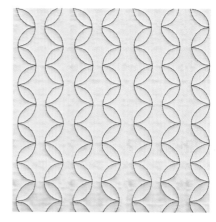

5. Place the straight base of the template against the tops of the half-circles of the first row, with the arrows parallel to the intersections touching the base. Stitch, and then reverse the template as before for the next row.

6. Repeat these rows across the space to create a pleasant directional pattern.

This design can also be used to create alternating mirror-imaged rows of stitching. Place the straight base of the template against the tops of the half-circles of the first row, with the arrows parallel to the intersections not touching the base. Stitch, and then reverse the template as before for the next row.

Leafy Waves

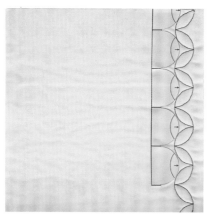

1. Follow Steps 1–4 for Linked Leaves (pages 52 and 53).

2. Bring the curve of the Clamshell template down in between the curves of the stitching, as shown in the photo, so it almost touches the previous stitching. Stitch along the scalloped edge of the template with a free-motion foot and the feed dogs down.

3. Rotate the template and place it so the arrows are on the points of the previous stitching. Stitch.

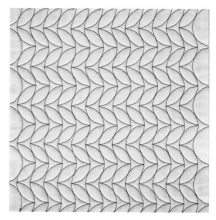

4. Repeat to fill the area. This creates a pattern with a lot of movement.

Filigree

This pattern uses the same two rows of stitching that make up Linked Leaves (page 52), but the way they are staggered changes everything.

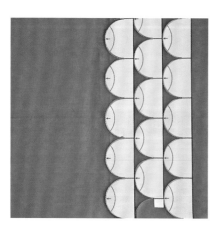

1. Follow Step 2 of Structured Clamshell Leaves (page 47) to make the template. I used several Clamshell templates for this design.

2. Make vertical and horizontal score lines across the center of the sample. Place the center template so the ends of the black arcs on the template are touching the vertical score line and a red arrow on the center clamshell is on the horizontal score line. Stagger the other templates so the red arrows touch the lines at the base.

3. Stitch along the scalloped edges of these templates with a free-motion foot and the feed dogs down.

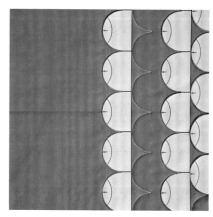

4. Remove 1 or more templates and put them in position for the next row. Stitch.

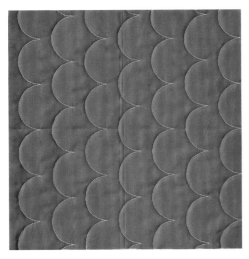

5. Continue filling the sample with these rows.

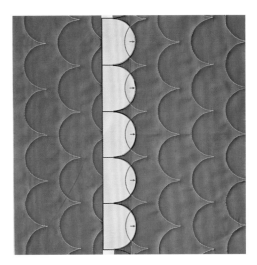

6. Rotate a template and place it so the black arcs on the template match the center row of stitching.

7. Stitch along the edge of the template (shown in red for illustration purposes).

8. Continue staggering the rows of stitching to create a filigree design.

Whirlpools

When I saw this pattern printed on batik fabric, I just had to see if I could duplicate it in quilting lines. This pattern is quite easy to create as long as the templates are placed correctly. It uses the Whirlpool template (page 58).

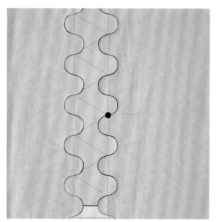

1. Make a vertical score line across the center of the sample. Make a small horizontal score line across the center to create a center point.

2. See Pattern Templates (page 11) for guidance in making the Whirlpool templates (page 58). Cut out at least 3 templates.

3. Place a template so the lines that divide the curves into half-circles are on top of the vertical score line and a triangle point is on the short horizontal score line. This is a pivot point (shown with a black dot).

4. Stitch on both sides of the template with a free-motion foot and the feed dogs down.

5. Add another template on each side of the first template and stitch on the outside edges of the added templates.

6. Continue moving the templates to the outside of the rows already created until the area has been filled. The pivot point should be at the center.

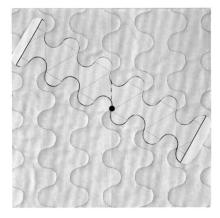 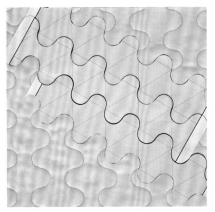 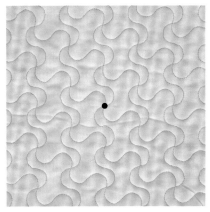

7. Rotate the template counterclockwise and position it as shown. Make sure the triangle points all match the lines of previous stitching on both sides of the template and a triangle leg is on top of the vertical score line. Stitch on both sides of the template.

8. Add another template on each side of the first template and stitch on the outside edges of the added templates.

9. Continue moving the templates to the outside of the rows already created until the area has been filled.

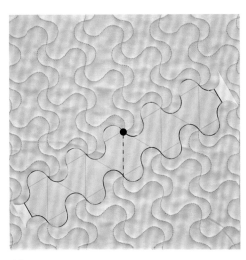 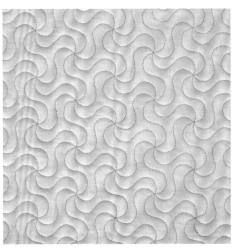

10. Rotate the template counterclockwise and position it as shown. Make sure the triangle points all match the intersections of previous rows of stitching on both sides of the template and a triangle leg is on top of the vertical score line, as shown in the photo. Stitch on both sides of the template.

11. Continue moving the templates to the outside of the rows already created until the sample is filled with this third line of stitching.

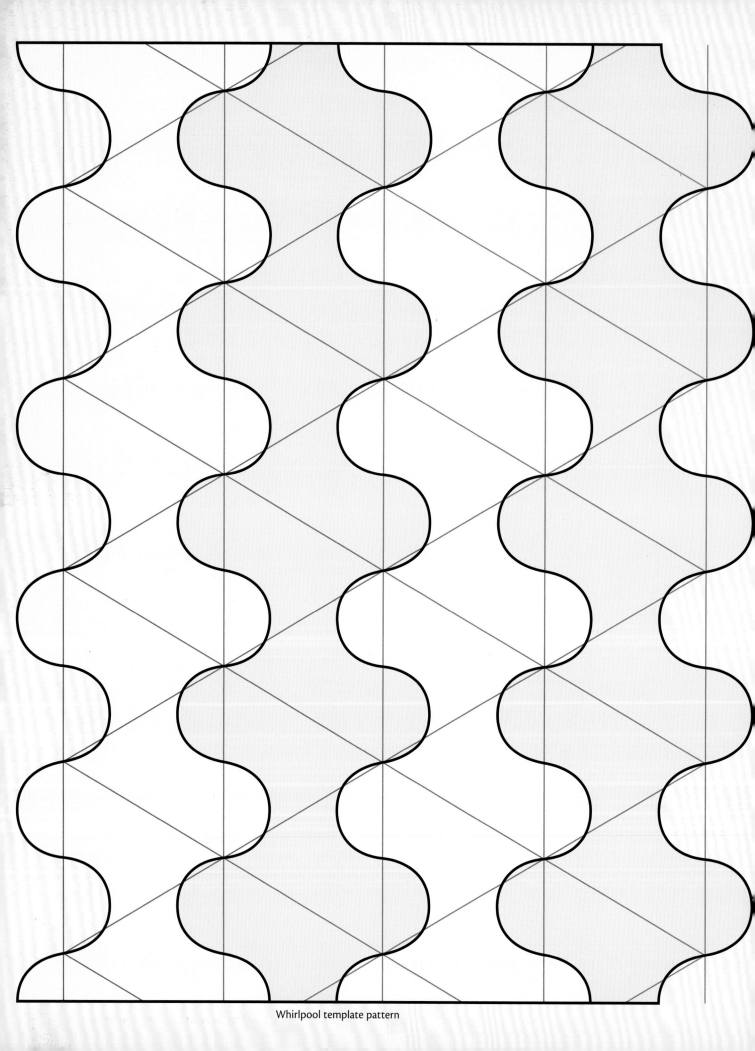

Whirlpool template pattern

CHAPTER 9

The Sinuous Curve Template

I like this template so much it gets its very own chapter. I've come up with several patterns that use it, and if I played around a bit longer I could probably come up with more.

Fish Net

The resulting pattern looks like netting or perhaps reptile scales.

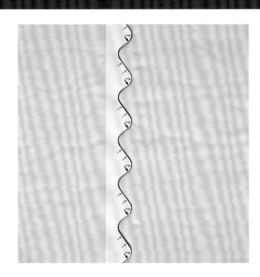

1. Make a vertical score line across the center of the sample.

2. See Pattern Templates (page 11) for guidance in making the Sinuous Curve template (page 61). Then, cut out 2 templates on the black line. You can use either the orange or the lavender template, or, for this pattern, you can use a white edge template.

3. Position the template along the vertical score line with the red arrows touching the line.

4. Stitch along the curved edge of the template with a free-motion foot and the feed dogs down.

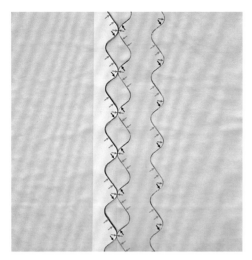

5. Place the other template so that its red arrows match the red arrows on the first template. Stitch along the left edge of the second template.

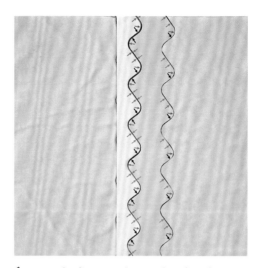

6. Move the first template so that the edges meet the second template.

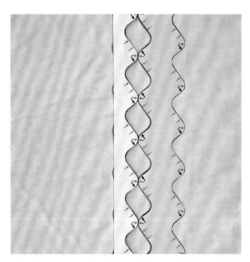

7. Move the second template so that the red arrows are matching again. Stitch along the left edge of the second template. This is the curved version of leap-frogging; matching and moving the templates places the next stitching line without measuring or marking.

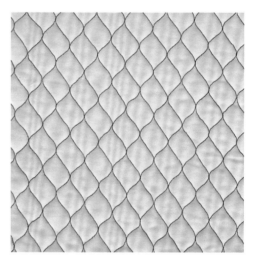

8. Continue placing the templates and stitching in this manner out to an edge of the sample and then turn and stitch to the other edge.

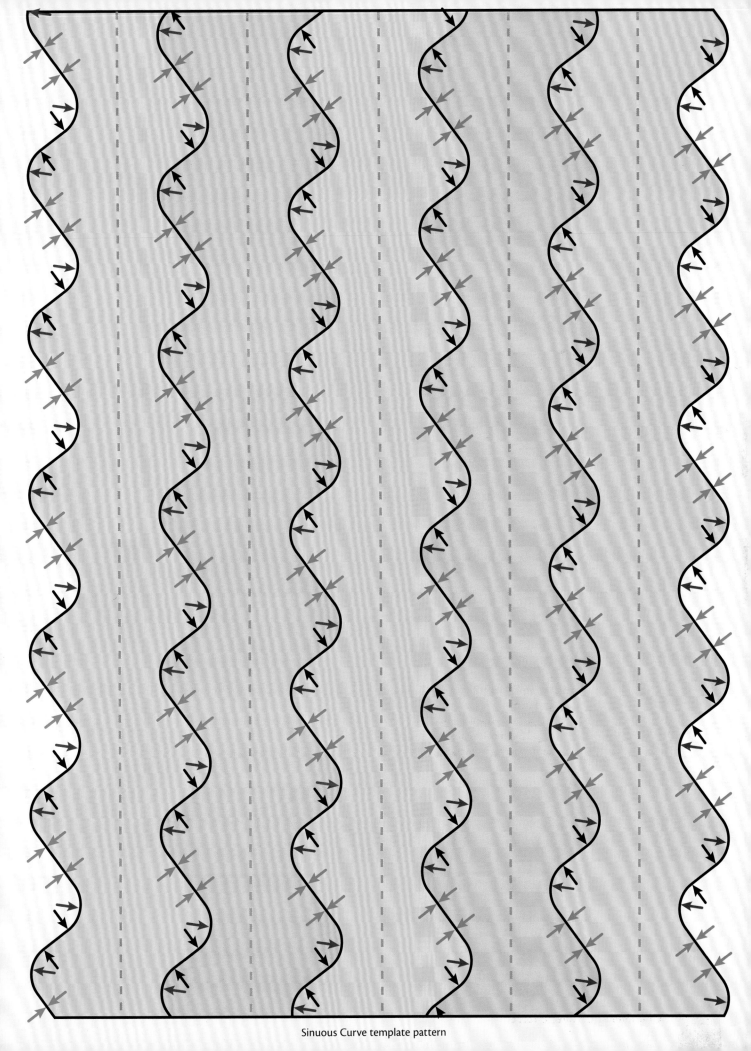

Sinuous Curve template pattern

Woven Beads

This pattern looks like seed beads that have been woven together.

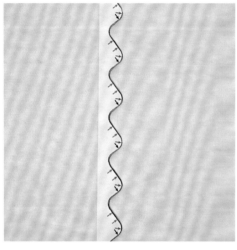

1. Make a vertical score line across the center of the sample.

2. See Pattern Templates (page 11) for guidance in making the Sinuous Curve template (page 61) and cut out 1 template on the black line.

3. Position the template on the fabric along the vertical score line so the black arrows are touching the line.

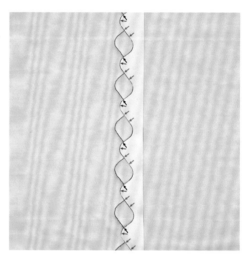

4. Stitch along the curved edge of the template with a free-motion foot and the feed dogs down.

5. Rotate the template and place it so the black arrow and the green arrow that is closest to the top of the curve match the previous row of stitching.

6. Stitch along the curved edge of the template.

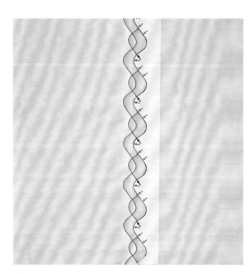

7. Move the template and place it so the black arrow and top green arrow match the previous row of stitching. Stitch along the curved edge of the template.

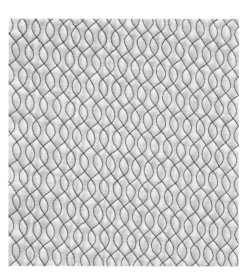

8. Continue moving the templates and stitching in this manner out to an edge of the sample and then turn and stitch to the other edge.

Tendrils

This pattern is a variation on the Woven Beads design and is stitched in sets of 4 rows. I think this pattern looks like locks of long hair after they have been curled.

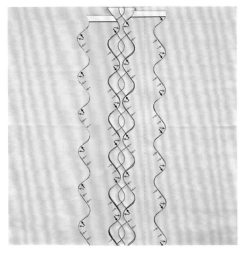

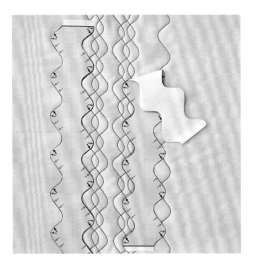

1. Complete Steps 1–6 for Woven Beads (page 62) to complete the first 2 rows of stitching. There will be 2 rows of stitching right on top of the score line.

2. Place 2 templates so the black and green arrows match the previous rows of stitching. Stitch on the inside edge of the templates to make a group of 4 stitched lines.

3. Stitch on the outside edge of the templates to place the next set of lines.

4. Place the templates and stitch to make another group of 4 stitched lines.

5. Remove the template, match it to the outer line of this group of 4 rows, and stitch another line that begins another group. The lavender template shows that the first line of a set of 4 has been stitched and is in place for the second line back toward the center. The orange template shows the placement to begin a new group of lines.

6. Stitch on the edge of the orange template and stitch 3 more lines back toward the center.

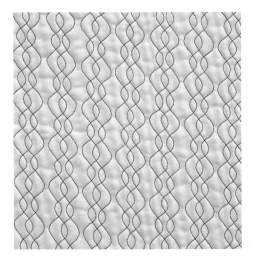

7. Continue placing the templates and stitching in this manner out to an edge of the sample and then turn and stitch to the other edge.

Tightly Twisted

This pattern is simply a matter of repeating the curve of the template over and over. But this quilting really gives an intriguing texture to the surface. It looks like rows of tightly twisted ropes placed side by side.

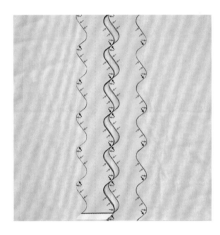

1. Make a horizontal score line across the center of the sample.

2. See Pattern Templates (page 11) for guidance in making the Sinuous Curve template (page 61) and cut out 2 templates on the black line. You can use either the orange or the lavender template, or, for this pattern, you can use a white edge template.

3. Position the template on the horizontal score line so the black arrows are touching the line. Place the other template so its black arrows match the black arrows on the first template.

4. Stitch along the inside edges of both of the templates with a free-motion foot and the feed dogs down.

5. Move the first template so the edges meet the second template.

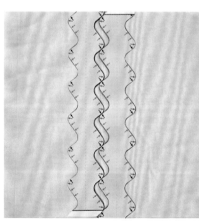

6. Move the second template so the black arrows are matching again; stitch along the edge of the second template.

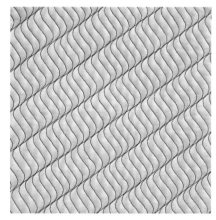

7. Continue placing the templates and stitching in this manner out to an edge of the sample and then turn and stitch to the other edge.

Ribbons

This is the easiest of the patterns to be made with the Sinuous Curve template.

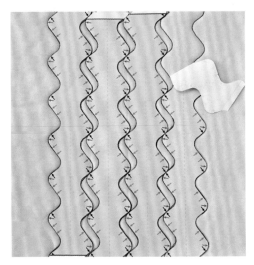

1. Make a vertical score line across the center of the sample.

2. See Pattern Templates (page 11) for guidance in making the Sinuous Curve template (page 61) and cut out 4 templates on the black line. You can use either the orange or the lavender template; don't use the white edge template for this pattern.

3. Position the template on the fabric on the vertical score line so that the black arrows are touching the score line. Place the other template so its black arrows match the black arrows on the first template. Stitch along the inside edge of both templates with a free motion foot and the feed dogs down.

4. Place the other 2 templates on the outside edges of the first 2 templates, matching the black arrows. Stitch along both edges of these new templates.

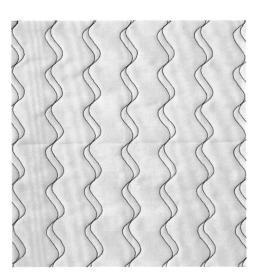

5. Remove the inner templates and place them on the outside. Stitch to form more rows of this double line. Continue until the space is filled with these double lines and ribbons twist across the sample.

Waves

Let's elaborate on the previous pattern. Add another wave line to each side of each double wave line. When placed horizontally, this design looks like a series of waves.

1. Follow Steps 1–5 for Ribbons (page 65).

2. Place a template so it matches an outside edge of the middle ribbon but also covers it. Stitch along the other edge. Take another template and match the black arrows to the edge that is matched to the stitching. Stitch along this edge.

3. Repeat, adding a line on each side of the ribbon so each ribbon becomes a group of 4 lines.

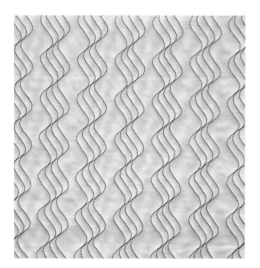

4. Continue until the space is filled.

Ribbon Plaid

The curving horizontal double lines intertwine to form a sort of plaid.

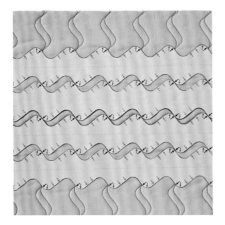

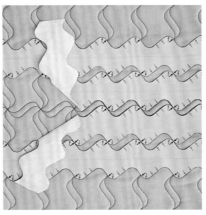

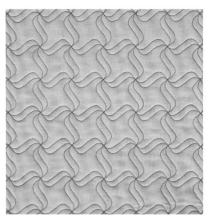

1. Follow Steps 1–5 for Ribbons (page 65).

2. Make a horizontal score line across the center of the sample.

3. Rotate the sample and position the templates beginning at the horizontal score line. Place the template so the black arrows are on the score line and match the narrowest part of the vertical ribbons. The outer edge of the template should also match the narrowest part of the vertical ribbons. Place another template so that its black arrows match the black arrows on the first template; check the outside edge of this template as well. Then add 2 more templates to either side. Notice that no thread shows in the gaps between the templates.

4. Stitch along both edges of the templates with a free-motion foot and the feed dogs down (red).

5. Continue moving the templates and stitching until the space is filled.

Now this is a fantastic pattern but, again, it can be taken even further.

Note

At this point, the quilting may have compacted the quilt sandwich somewhat. You may need to pull the fabric a bit or squish the template together to make the arrows fit.

Whirligigs

This design will look like endless spinning whirligigs. This mind-boggling design is created by adding another staggered layer of Ribbon Plaid over the first layer. This is, arguably, the most difficult pattern in the book, but the surface looks almost alive. Since the quilt sandwich has been compacted so much already, greater care will be needed to help the templates fit.

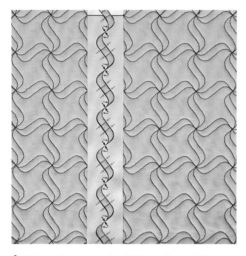

1. Follow Steps 1–5 for Ribbons (page 65).

2. Follow Steps 2–5 for Ribbon Plaid (page 67).

3. Cut on the dotted line on the template to divide it in half; this helps compensate for the compaction of the quilting.

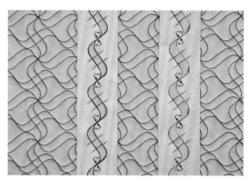

4. Place the straight edge of the template on the intersections of the Ribbon Plaid design that are on the score line. Match the green arrows to the stitching lines of the ribbons as shown. Match the black arrows on the other half of the divided template to the half already in place. Stitch along the curved edges of each half-template.

Note

When the templates are correctly placed, the only stitching that should show is the 2 lines that match the green arrows. Notice in this photo that the templates on the right have a bit of previous stitching showing in the curves. This is problematic and the template should be adjusted.

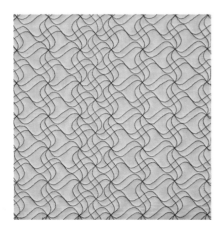

5. Repeat with every vertical space between the Ribbon Plaid, placing the straight edge of the half-template on the intersections of the Ribbon Plaid, and matching the green arrows to the rows of stitching. Repeat for the horizontal spaces.

6. Continue moving the templates and stitching until the space is filled.

CHAPTER 10

Expanding the Options

One of the easiest ways of changing the patterns in this book is to change the scale of the design. All the template designs can be easily enlarged or reduced by using those functions on a photocopy machine or printer. If you want to do the Filigree pattern (page 54) in a 3″-wide border, enlarge the Clamshell template by 200%. If you really want to give yourself a challenge, reduce the Sinuous Curve template by 50% and make the Whirligigs pattern with all those tiny little swirls. (Come on—I dare ya!)

Other changes can be made by spacing the lines farther apart. This brings up that four-letter word MATH. It's not so bad, though; you only need to do the simplest of addition and/or multiplication or use percentages, as in the examples above. As discussed in Herringbone (page 18), variations can be created by changing the width of the masking tape being used. If you have a utilitarian quilt you want to finish quickly, use 2″-wide masking tape for the first Variation on V (page 18). Structured Clamshell Leaves (page 47) and Structured Orange Peel (page 49) each have two elements to the pattern. If you decide to enlarge either pattern by half, you would need to enlarge the template by 150% and stitch the grid with the lines spaced 1½″ apart.

The Enhanced Grid patterns (pages 44–51) can be stitched on rectangles instead of squares. For example, make the vertical lines 1″ apart and the horizontal lines 1¼″ apart for an elongated look. Or, try using a 45° or 60° diamond grid for a really skewed design.

Inchie Ruler Tape does not have to be used only in the way it's been cut—1″ strips. If a precise 2″-wide strip is needed, use clear tape to attach 2 strips together before peeling them off the backing paper. If a thinner strip is needed, use your rotary cutter and ruler to cut a strip in half or even in quarters. Of course, you should do this before peeling off the backing paper.

Fractured Star

Here's a pattern that uses full pieces of Inchie Ruler Tape but then changes when half-width pieces are used.

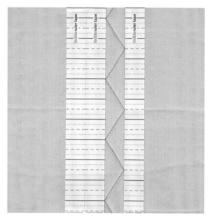

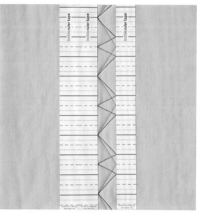

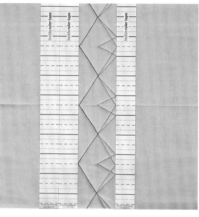

1. Make vertical and horizontal score lines across the center of the sample.

2. Place a piece of Inchie Ruler Tape with an edge on the vertical score line. Add a piece of tape to each side. Remove the middle piece to create a 1″-wide work area. Place the middle piece on the outside of one of the other pieces of tape.

3. The point of a zigzag needs to be centered on the horizontal score line. Count back from the center to find a starting point and then begin stitching diagonally across 1½″ back and forth to complete the first row.

4. For the second row of stitching, stitch diagonally across 1″, then back diagonally ½″, then back diagonally ½″, then back diagonally 1″ to complete the 3″ repeat that overlays the first large zigzag (red) as shown. It looks like an M or a W, depending which way you look at it. Repeat to complete the second row of stitching (blue).

5. Remove the center-left piece of tape and place it to the outside left to reveal a new working area. Stitch the large 1½″ zigzag in mirror image, matching the points from the previous row (blue).

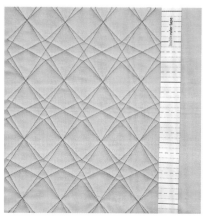

6. Repeat the second row of irregular zigzag in mirror image (purple).

7. Continue moving the tape and stitching until the space has been filled.

Note

If you look at these 4 zigzag lines as a unit, you will see that several of the straight lines that were made in 2 parts could have perhaps been made more easily if worked on a 2″-wide work area. I did try it this way, but I found that I had to think a lot harder about which mark on the tape I would stitch to, and that when I made these longer lines I didn't stitch them quite as straight. However, there is less pivoting if you use the 2″ area. If you can see the structure of the pattern, it can be worked on a 2″-wide area. I found it easier to work the pattern 1″ at a time.

Changing Tape Width

I have left an area of the sample open to show how the design can be changed by changing the width of the tape.

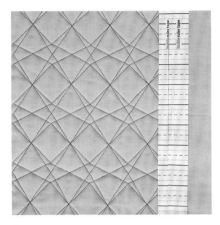

1. Cut a piece of Inchie Ruler Tape in half lengthwise to make a piece that is ½″ wide. Place it next to the remaining piece of tape.

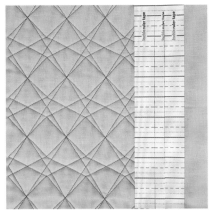

2. Place a 1″ piece of tape on the other side of the ½″ piece.

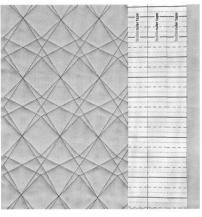

3. Remove the original piece as well as the ½″ piece. Then, place 2 more full pieces to the right of the remaining piece.

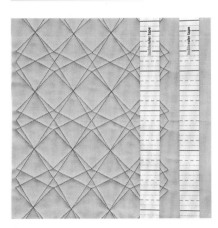

4. Remove the middle piece. Half of this new work area will be filled with stitching from the previous rows.

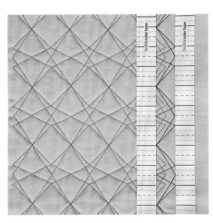

5. Stitch the 2 rows of zigzag as shown by the purple stitching.

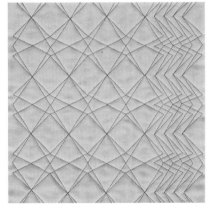

6. Use the ½″ piece to space the next work area, as explained above, moving to the right. Repeat until several same-direction rows have been made.

Note

This version of the pattern is very dense but would make a fabulous border. Or, if you were really determined, it would make an interesting background fill.

This pattern is a great example of how a design can be changed by varying the width of the tape used.

CHAPTER II

Pattern Placement and Planning
A Quilt in the Works

I'd like to show the process I went through in quilting a challenge piece I did for the Road to California Quilt Conference. The goal of the challenge was to show how quilting really can make the difference in a quilt. I don't know how many identical quilt tops were made, but I agreed to be one of the participants and I decided to quilt my top with patterns from this book.

I had no idea what sort of top I would receive, but when I opened the package there was a huge star on a blue background.

Blue and Yellow Star

First, I measured the piece. The borders and the background were even or close to even numbers—very fortunate for me. I basted the quilt and then, using a walking foot, did outline stitching on all the piecing lines to stabilize the quilt. (The basting mostly holds the quilt in place, but it's still loose enough that some slight shifting may take place. The outline stitching keeps each area contained.)

Borders

I decided to work from the border inward, so I measured the border from corner to corner of the yellow sashing, ignoring the corners of the border for the time being—it was 28″ × 4¼″.

I chose the Serpentine Zigzag I pattern (page 23) for the border areas. I began by finding the center of the border, 14″, and placed a pin there.

Then, I cut Inchie Ruler Tape into 4¼″-long pieces and used 4 of those. I placed 1 on each side of the center pin and 1 on each side of those, with the ¼″ end of the tape next to the sashing. Next, I removed the piece to the right of the pin and placed that piece to the left, leaving a work area.

One of the reasons I chose the Serpentine Zigzag I was that I knew if I started in the right place I could stitch to the edge of the sashing, then turn around and come back. This way, I wouldn't have thread ends to tie in along the border. The ¼″ piece of tape on the sashing would give me space to turn around. I figured out where I would need to start and used inch marks and quarter-inch marks to stitch the row.

1 row of Serpentine Zigzag I

Left side of border complete

Next, I removed the tape to the left of the pin and worked a mirror-image row.

2 rows of Serpentine Zigzag I

I used my fourth piece of tape and covered the row that was just sewn, then stitched a row just like the row the tape covered. I continued leapfrogging the tape to the left until I reached the corner of the sashing.

Then I repeated the mirror-image row out to the right corner. I repeated this on the other 3 sides. Finally, I stitched crosshatching in the corners to finish the border.

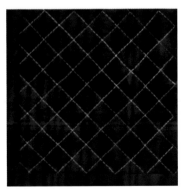

Border corner

Background

The Fractured Star pattern (page 70) seemed suitable for the background behind the yellow star, which measured 26″. This pattern needed to be worked around the star, and I wanted it to come out symmetrically. It's also a directional pattern, which added complexity to the planning. I deciding that dividing the quilt in half was to my advantage, so I placed blue masking tape across the middle to indicate the center. I then joined Inchie Ruler Tape to make 4 pieces 13½″ long and placed them in the center of half the star, with ½″ overlapping the sashing.

In my instructions for the Fractured Star I began with the easier zigzag line, but for this quilt I decided it would work better to stitch the irregular zigzag lines and then go back and put the easier lines over the top. So, I drew the zigzag on the tape.

I drew the design the whole length of the tape, but the only parts I stitched were the blue background. I proceeded to leapfrog the pieces of tape—first to the left and then to the right. I kept measuring how many inches I had left as I moved outward and found that I was gaining space. I compensated by adding a fraction of an inch between the pieces of tape rather than butting them up against each other.

Once the first half was finished, I started working on the second half, moving from the outside to the center, so I could match up the rows on the side. It all matched up beautifully, and I used only 8 pieces of tape to do the background—4 for each side. At this point the design looks like a bunch of wonky 4-sided shapes.

Then, I went back and did the easier zigzag stitching, matching the lines to the appropriate corners.

Fractured Star background

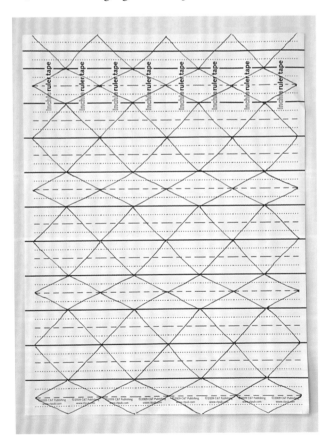

Eight pieces of tape with design

Star

I stitched the star by making straight lines that connect and turn into crosshatching and then connect across the corners of the inner star to form a snowflake-like pattern. I used Inchie Ruler Tape to stitch the small zigzag in the sashing.

I do hope that while reading the details of the quilting process for this quilt, ideas have sprung into your head on how you can use the patterns in this book in your own work.

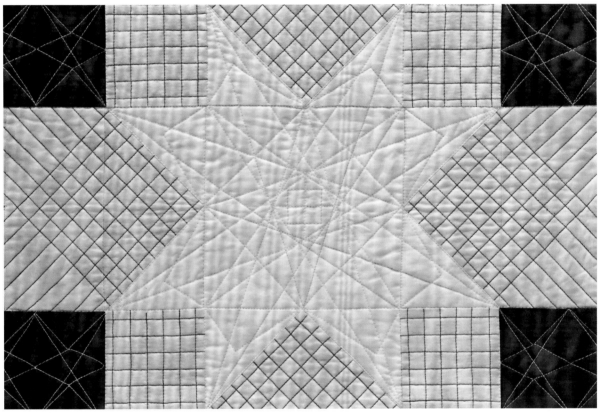

Straight-line quilting in star

Gallery

Tree Perspective by Lisa Chin

This abstract landscape gains a touch of the familiar through the use of Darts to create tall trees.

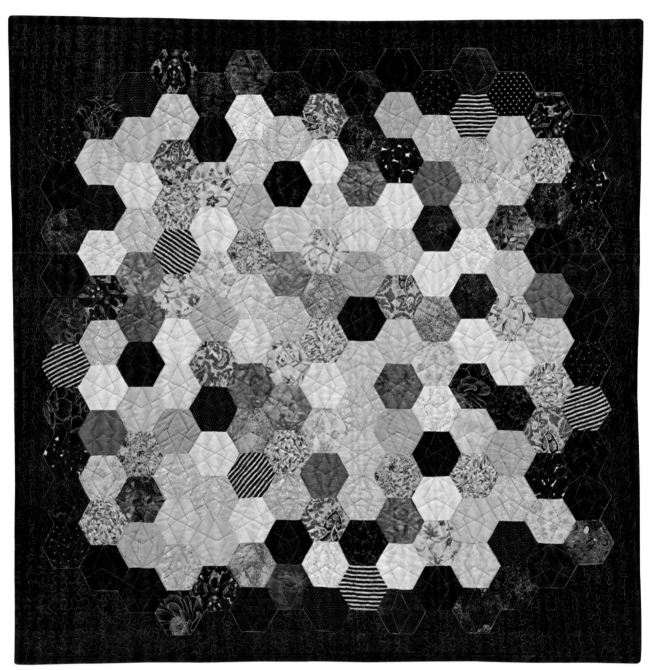

Red & Yellow Hexagons by Cathy Sandman

The Double X pattern was reformatted by Cathy to fit the hexagons in this colorful quilt.

Love Gardens by Cyndy Ward

Cyndy made this lovely quilt using the BQ2 pattern from Maple Island Quilts and then quilted it using designs from *One Line at a Time*.

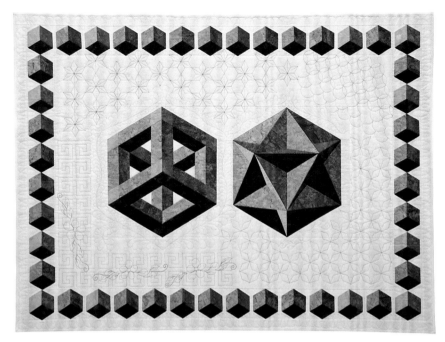

Floating Hexagons by Cory Weir

Using a block from Jinny Beyer's *Quilter's Album of Patchwork Patterns,* Corinna designed a quilt with lots of open space for quilting. She used several patterns from *One Line at a Time* and the Diamond Plaid pattern from this book.

Noah and Friends by Cyndy Ward

The background of the blocks in this quilt is delightfully filled with geometric patterns.

Montana Barn by Ann Breznock

Ann mostly completed this quilt top in a class taught by Georgia Bonesteel at the Cowgirl Quilter Retreat at the Nine Quarter Circle Ranch. She kindly agreed to quilt it using my designs and chose to use Squares & Diamonds for the barn roof and sky and Darts for the border.

Card Trick by Janet Coleman

Intertwined Stars, Variations on V, and Ohio Star patterns were used to quilt this lovely traditional piece.

Nine Patch Parade by Kathy King

The background of this lovely traditional piece is filled with the Ohio Star quilting pattern.

Hearts from Africa by Kathy King

Featuring a hand-painted African fabric panel, Kathy framed the piece with patchwork. She then used Darts in the border, Diamond Plaid in the background, and a Variation on V for the white shrub.

Flower Wreath by Lisa Chin

The Filigree pattern was used to quilt the border in this sweet piece.

Ribbon of Rainbow by Holly Haugen

The black background on this quilt features a variation using the Clamshell template.

Hunting Wildlife by Holly Haugen

Warm and cuddly, this flannel quilt uses Variations on V, Darts, and Holly's take on the Serpentine Zigzag.

Jacket by Kelly Kelsey

This cozy jacket employs three of the designs from this book. Kelly did the quilting, first stitching through the top fabric and batting but not the backing. The yoke has Diamond Plaid, the body has Darts, and the sleeves have Intertwined Stars. Once the quilting was done the jacket pattern pieces were cut out and the garment was assembled with an independent lining to cover the batting.

Weaving World Peace by Masuda Medcalf

Masuda quilted the center of this quilt, which is based on a Navajo blanket, with many of the patterns in this book. But she decided to try hand quilting the borders—something you could do with any of these patterns. She used a zigzag that turns into Rolling X in two of the corners.

Going Green by Beverly Hunnicutt

Beverly used several patterns from *One Line at a Time* and did the quilting on this large quilt using a 50-year-old domestic machine.

The Dancer by Teresa Darr

Teresa took a Pieced Pictures class from me and created this top from a kit I provided.
Then she took my Machine Quilting class and used some of the patterns she learned to enhance the wallhanging.

Takeout for Two by Beverly Hart

This clever Asian-themed quilt features geometric patterns in the quilting.

Happy Haunting by Shanna Werner

Shanna used Darts modified to fit the size of the border and a wonky version
of Squares & Diamonds that fits the Halloween feeling quite well.

Thoughts of Spring by Lisa Brothman

Structured Orange Peel fills the center of this small quilt, which was enhanced with metallic inks after quilting. Lisa also made Variations on V run four directions and fit the border perfectly.

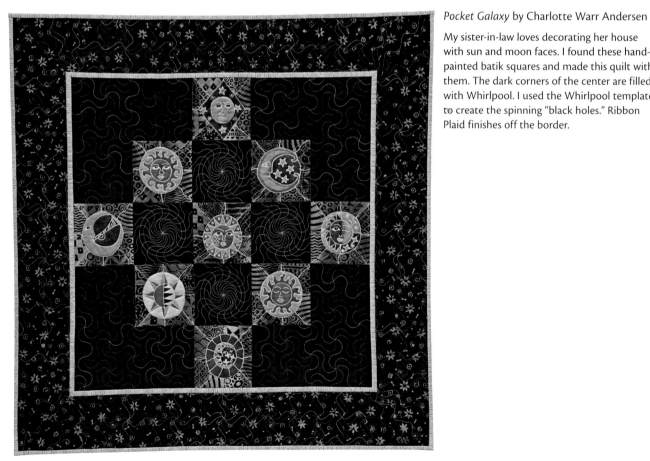

Pocket Galaxy by Charlotte Warr Andersen

My sister-in-law loves decorating her house with sun and moon faces. I found these hand-painted batik squares and made this quilt with them. The dark corners of the center are filled with Whirlpool. I used the Whirlpool template to create the spinning "black holes." Ribbon Plaid finishes off the border.

Autumn Table Runner by Lisa Brothman

Each large square of this table runner contains a different pattern from the book.

Detail of *Family Crest Alzheimer's Name Quilt*

Family Crest Alzheimer's Name Quilt
by Charlotte Warr Andersen

The Alzheimer's Art Quilt Initiative headed by Ami Simms has been collecting names handwritten on purple swatches of fabric. These swatches have been stitched into scores of oddly shaped quilts 6 inches wide by 6 or more feet long. I was privileged to quilt two of these pieces. This one features digitized Japanese family crests surrounded by the Squares & Diamonds quilting pattern.

Sampler Alzheimer's Name Quilt
by Charlotte Warr Andersen

This narrow quilt was randomly divided into sections and different quilting patterns from this book were used in each section.

In Anticipation—Inauguration Day by Charlotte Warr Andersen

I was assigned this event for an invitational show with the theme "America Celebrates."
I hope that one day we do have a woman as U.S. president. The border features Darts.

Photo by Ken Sanville Photography

HMQS "Sew Batik" Quilting Challenge by Brenda Bell

In winning second place in this challenge, Brenda skillfully used Whirling Stars from *One Line at a Time* and Diamond Plaid at half-scale, and embellished the intersections with crystals.

About the Author

Charlotte Warr Andersen is an avid and well-known quilter. A native Utahn, she was born in Salt Lake City and has lived there all her life. She learned many needle skills from her mother, but she considers most of her quilting skills to be self-taught or acquired by good observation. Having recently become an empty nester, she resides with her husband, Eskild, and two dogs, Hugo and Legion. Stitching a portrait is still one of her favorite pastimes.

Charlotte travels and teaches her stitching and quilting methods. She served as president of the International Quilt Association for two terms, from 2006 to 2009.

Now that the children have all moved out, she may have room to purchase a longarm machine. But at the time of the completion of this book, she was still doing all her own quilting on her Berninas.

Previous books by Charlotte Warr Andersen:

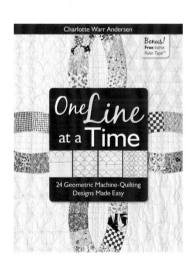

Great Titles and Tools *from* C&T PUBLISHING and STASH BOOKS

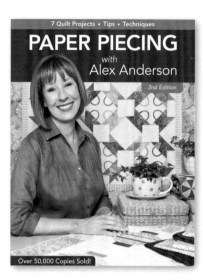

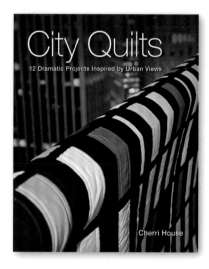

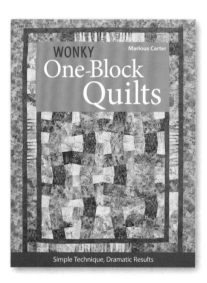

Available at your local retailer or **www.ctpub.com** *or* **800-284-1114**

For a list of other fine books from C&T Publishing, visit our website to view our catalog online.

C&T PUBLISHING, INC.
P.O. Box 1456
Lafayette, CA 94549
800-284-1114

Email: ctinfo@ctpub.com
Website: www.ctpub.com

C&T Publishing's professional photography services are now available to the public. Visit us at www.ctmediaservices.com.

Tips and Techniques can be found at www.ctpub.com > Consumer Resources > Quiltmaking Basics: Tips & Techniques for Quiltmaking & More

For quilting supplies:

COTTON PATCH
1025 Brown Ave.
Lafayette, CA 94549
Store: 925-284-1177
Mail order: 925-283-7883

Email: CottonPa@aol.com
Website: www.quiltusa.com

Note: Fabrics used in the quilts shown may not be currently available, as fabric manufacturers keep most fabrics in print for only a short time.